MIA: Missing In Action

MIA: missing in action

A Vietnam Drama
by Edward F. Dolan

Franklin Watts / 1989
New York / London / Toronto / Sydney

Photographs courtesy of: UPI/Bettmann Newsphotos: pp. 8, 32, 33, 53, 65 (top), 81; AP/Wide World Photos: pp. 29, 45, 69, 71 (both), 102, 105; Magnum: p. 65 (bottom, Paul Fusco).

Library of Congress Cataloging-in-Publication Data
Dolan, Edward F., 1924–
Missing in action : a Vietnam drama / by Edward F. Dolan.
p. cm.
Bibliography: p.
Includes index.
Summary: Discusses the mysterious disappearance of thousands of American servicemen serving in Vietnam and other areas of Southeast Asia during the years of war and turmoil in that region. Examines the issue of government reluctance to support the efforts to rescue and help find these missing men.
ISBN 0-531-10665-9
1. Vietnamese Conflict, 1961–1975—Missing in action—United States—Juvenile literature. [1. Vietnamese Conflict. 1961–1975—Missing in action.] I. Title.
DS559.8.M5D65 1989
959.704'33'73—dc19 88-31373 CIP AC

CONTENTS

I am indebted to many people for their assistance during the preparation of this book. In particular, for providing me with much research material, I wish to express my appreciation to the following organizations: National League of Families of American Prisoners and Missing in Southeast Asia (NLF); Red Badge of Courage, Inc.; and National Vietnam Veterans Coalition.

A very special word of thanks must go to Colleen Shine, Public Affairs Coordinator with the NLF, and Adrian Fisch, Director of Red Badge of Courage. Both were more than helpful in answering specific questions and helping me trace needed material.

Finally, my appreciation to Patricia K. Lane for her review of my manuscript and her helpful comments.

Introduction
THE MISSING
OF VIETNAM

The Vietnam War exacted a terrible cost in human life for all the nations that fought in it. For the United States, the toll added up to more than 55,000 servicemen killed, 153,000 wounded, and upwards of 3,000 listed as missing in action.[1] This book is about those missing Americans—Americans who disappeared in battles, ambushes, and air crashes.

They stand at the center of a national drama that began in 1973 and has continued to this very day. In the proceeding pages, we'll see the drama unfolding through the years, revealing itself as a story of mystery, frustration, and angry controversy as the U.S. government and concerned Americans everywhere have sought not only to learn what happened to the men and women missing in action (MIAs) but also to find them and, whether they are dead or somehow still alive, bring them home.

To understand fully this drama and the reasons why it has persisted for more than two decades, we need to know something of the background against which it has been played. We need to know something of the Vietnam War itself.

In 1954, after eight years of fighting, the forces of the communist leader Ho Chi Minh drove the French out of Vietnam. A foreign domination was ended that had begun a century earlier. However, although Vietnam was now an independent nation, it was anything but a unified one.

The nation was sharply divided into two political factions—the communists and the noncommunists. The communists, headquartered in the city of Hanoi, controlled the northern half of the country. The noncommunists were strongly entrenched in the southern half; their capital city was Saigon. Though the communists and noncommunists dominated the scene, they were opposed by various groups in their respective areas. For example, there were strong northern supporters in the south. Many of their number made up the fighting force known as the Vietcong.

So sharply opposed were the two factions that the job of establishing a government in which both could participate was out of the question. Consequently, an international conference held in Geneva, Switzerland, in 1954 tried to solve the matter by dividing the country into two states—North and South Vietnam. The division was made along a line at the 17th Parallel, with the northern lands going to the communists and the southern lands to the noncommunists.

The division, however, was planned as a temporary one. The conference declared that the country would be reunified in a free election scheduled for 1956. In the two-year interim, the Vietnamese people were to look at both the North and South Vietnamese governments and choose which should govern the country as a whole. Then they would vote accordingly.

As matters turned out, the people never got a chance to go to the polls, because in 1955 the southern leader Ngo Ninh Diem declared his state to be an independent nation. He took this step in an attempt to overwhelm the opposition shown to

his government by various factions in the south. Then he announced that the newly formed country, which he called the Republic of South Vietnam, would have nothing to do with the election but would go its own way.

The North Vietnamese government was enraged by this turn of events; warfare broke out between the two states. For the most part, the communist side of the fighting was initially carried out by a guerrilla force in the south, the Vietcong. (Its full name was Viet Nam Cong San, meaning the Vietnamese communists.) Diem's army fared so poorly against the Vietcong fighters and then the North Vietnamese troops that joined them in increasing numbers through the years that he asked the United States for both military *and* financial aid. The United States had been giving the southern government financial aid ever since Vietnam had been divided into two states.

Though knowing his regime to be corrupt and tyrannical, the United States agreed to provide Diem with the requested aid because, as unsavory as he might be, he was an anticommunist and was fighting against communism, a political ideology that the United States had long opposed. It was for the very same reason that the United States had given Saigon economic aid during the period in which the Vietnamese unification election was planned. Military equipment and supplies began to arrive in 1961. Also arriving on the scene were small contingents of U.S. servicemen. Called "advisers," their job was to help train the South Vietnamese army.

The fighting between the north and south intensified in the next years. At every turn along the way, the Vietcong and the North Vietnamese troops proved themselves far deadlier than Diem's forces. Consequently, the United States gave more and more military assistance to the South Vietnamese cause. Air force planes began to bomb North Vietnam in retaliation for the growing number of communist troops being dispatched south across the 17th Parallel. Then the United States began to contribute not advisers but fighting troops to the conflict.

The number of troops increased steadily as the fighting raged on, growing to 180,000 by the end of 1965. The total jumped to about 400,000 in the next year. By 1969, more than half a million Americans had been committed to the fighting.

Early on, America's participation in the war caused much controversy at home. In the main, the first outcries against the United States's role were heard from the nation's young people. They opposed the very idea of war itself and resisted being drafted into the armed services and made to fight, and perhaps die, in a conflict that they saw as immoral and useless. They were at first widely condemned for their stance. In time, however, their opposition came to be shared by vast segments of the American public, and the Vietnam conflict came to be known as the most hated war in United States history.

The opposition to the war took many forms across the nation. There was sorrow for the sufferings of the Vietnamese civilians trapped in the fighting—sorrow for the deaths and injuries, the homes lost, the villages and fields destroyed—and the desire to see the horror stopped. There was worry over what the costs of the war were doing to the American economy; by the time all was said and done, the United States would pour a staggering $150 billion into the conflict, at one point spending $2 billion a month on the fighting. There was the sick fear that Agent Orange, the chemical being used by the air force to defoliate the Vietnamese jungles in an effort to unmask Vietcong hiding places, was poisoning the land, the Vietnamese people, and our own soldiers. And there was the awful pain of watching the toll of American deaths and injuries steadily increase.

The outcry reached such proportions, both at home and abroad, that the United States began a gradual withdrawal of its troops in 1969. Then, in 1973, upon the signing of a ceasefire pact with the North Vietnamese, all remaining U.S. troops departed.

It was then that the drama of the missing Americans of Vietnam took shape. It remains with us today, a story of mysteries, of frustration, and of angry controversy. In all, it is a sad reminder of the most hated conflict in U.S. history, a reminder that has been kept alive through the years much because the Vietnam War was so hated.

Chapter One
THE UNENDING
DRAMA

March 1967: U.S. Army Staff Sgt. Burt C. Small, Jr., is serving as an adviser to a South Vietnamese army unit on patrol in enemy territory. Suddenly, shots ring out from the surrounding underbrush. The sergeant falls with a bullet in his leg. His companions retreat and then watch as four North Vietnamese soldiers emerge from the foliage and lead Sergeant Small away. He is never seen again.

June 1969: Marine Capt. Walter R. Schmidt, Jr., takes to his parachute when his plane is shot down over South Vietnam. Upon landing, he radios his position to his base and says that his leg is broken. Enemy forces are sighted nearby during the time that a rescue team tries to reach him. The team finally arrives at the crash site. The captain has disappeared—for all time to come.

January 1973: Air Force Capt. Mark A. Peterson and his copilot both eject from their observation plane when enemy fire brings it down in South Vietnam. They are sighted from the air as their parachutes float earthward. As soon as they land, one of the men radios that he is about to be captured by the enemy. The two fliers vanish for good.[1]

These stories tell of four American servicemen who disappeared during the Vietnam War and were listed by the U.S. government as missing in action (MIA). They are but a handful of the nation's soldiers, sailors, airmen, and civilians whose fates were unknown in 1973, the year that marked the end of America's participation in the fighting. Altogether the U.S. Department of Defense listed between 2,400 and 2,500 Americans as MIA. Included on the list were 2 women, 110 black servicemen, and 42 civilians.

The missing Americans, long since known simply as MIAs, were lost not only in Vietnam itself. They also disappeared in the surrounding countries of Laos, Cambodia (now called Kampuchea), and China. Some 556 vanished in Laos, 82 in Cambodia, and 6 in China. Counted as lost inside North and South Vietnam—or in the waters off their coasts—were approximately 1,800 MIAs.[2]

A NATIONAL DRAMA

Their loss quickly led to a great national drama when the United States withdrew from the war. It was triggered by the deep desire of families of the MIAs and countless fellow Americans to learn what had happened to them. People throughout the country demanded to know if any of those lost were still alive and being held captive by the North Vietnamese. If so, they wanted the government to locate them and return them safely home. And they begged to know if the bodies of MIAs thought to be dead were being held in North Vietnam or its neighboring countries. If so, the government must have them released and brought home for burial.

Furthermore, the families and friends of those possibly dead wanted to know for sure that their loved ones had actually perished in the fighting. Only then could they put the agony of uncertainty over the fate of a father, a husband, a son, or a sweetheart behind them and continue their lives.

The MIA drama has continued through the years to this day and may extend well into the future before coming to an end. It is a story that contains many elements.

It is made up, first, of family griefs. Next, it has been marked from the beginning by often angry political negotiations between the United States and the North Vietnamese. Furthermore, it has been punctuated throughout with American accusations that the North Vietnamese are holding living and dead MIAs as hostages and will not release them until given billions of dollars in U.S. economic aid. Above all else, it has been a story filled with mysterious happenings, reports of captive MIAs still surviving in Southeast Asia,* searches for secret MIA prisons in jungles, and questions as to whether the remains of the few dead MIAs who have been returned to the United States are really those of the men they are said to be. Very often, those remains, especially the ones extracted from the scenes of air crashes, have been mere bits of bone.

How this drama, which has cast a shadow over the lives of millions of Americans, has unfolded through the long years since the Vietnam War ended is the subject of this book.

We must first, however, set the stage for the drama. To do so, we'll need to answer three questions:

- The term "missing in action" must be used in a special way when thinking of Vietnam. *Why?*

---

*The term "Southeast Asia" embraces a broad range of nations, among them Thailand, the Philippines, Malaysia, Brunei, Vietnam, Laos, and Cambodia. The countries discussed in this book—Vietnam, Laos, and Cambodia (Kampuchea)—technically are known together as "Indochina." In this book, they will be referred to as "Southeast Asia" when speaking of them as a group since "Southeast Asia" is the term most widely used in the press, in books, and by organizations involved in MIA work.

- It is suspected that some MIAs may still be alive in Southeast Asia even after so much time has passed since the war's end. *If so, how many might they number?*

- The widespread demand that the Vietnam MIAs, both living and dead, be found is considered unique in American history. *Why?*

MIA: A SPECIAL MEANING

Ordinarily, the term "missing in action" refers to wartime personnel who disappear in the fighting and whose fates are unknown to their government. This, however, is not the case with the Vietnam MIAs; they are divided into two types. The first of the two, consisting in great part of air-crash victims, does not fit the usual meaning given to MIA.

To see why this type doesn't fit, we need to know that at the time the United States was planning to leave Vietnam, the Department of Defense listed about 800 personnel as being either MIAs or prisoners of war (POWs). Then, just before the nation did depart, the department added a long series of names to the list. Chiefly added were the names of men who were thought to have been killed but whose bodies had never been found.[3] Among the additions were the victims of such air crashes as the following two:

At 8:30 on a December night in 1972, a B-52 bomber is hit by an antiaircraft missile. Rolling over, the ship plummets earthward and smashes into a tiny North Vietnamese village. As the plane falls, two crewmen jump clear. They parachute into the jungle, where they are captured by enemy troops (to be released some months later in an exchange of American and North Vietnamese prisoners). No trace is ever found of their four fellow crewmen who could not escape. It is presumed that they died in the crash.[4]

Later that same December, an AC-130 gunship is heading home to its base in Thailand after a mission over North Vietnam. The plane is struggling to stay aloft as it flies above a jungle area in Laos at sunset. Its fuel line has been punctured by enemy ground fire. Suddenly, the ship explodes in flames and dives into the ground. As had happened in the B-52 incident, two crewmen parachute to safety. But their fourteen comrades are unable to follow them out. The plane smashes in a giant cloud of fire and smoke. Rescuers make their way to the crash site the next day and find the remains of one man. All the other crewmen, a total of thirteen, have been incinerated or are buried deep in the smoking and twisted wreckage.[5]

When the additions were made to the MIA/POW list, they brought the number of prisoners and missing to between 3,100 and 3,200.*

Of that total, 591 men were POWs who were returned in an American–North Vietnamese prisoner exchange that took place immediately after the United States withdrew from the war. The exchange reduced the list to just above 2,500 men.† The Department of Defense then classified upwards of 2,400 of their number as actual MIAs. The remainder were designated as possible POWs or were given other classifications. Due to the circumstances under which they disappeared, such

---

*It may seem odd to be using general figures such as "between 3,100 and 3,200" and "between 2,400 and 2,500" when we might expect the government to have specific totals for the MIAs and POWs. The fact of the matter is that the exact number of names on the expanded list has always been a problem. When the Department of Defense compiled the list, the names were received from different sources, among them various intelligence agencies and the branches of the armed services. Because of clerical mix-ups and human error and because there was no central clearinghouse for the information at that time, an exact total for the list has never been established to the satisfaction of all concerned in locating the MIAs and POWs.[6]

†Over the years, many news reports on the MIA issue have confused readers. The reports have usually stated that upwards of 2,500 U.S. personnel are missing. This figure is puzzling because it differs from the tally of 2,400–2,500. The difference exists because in time *all* the people on the expanded list came to be widely called MIAs.

as artillery barrages and plane crashes, some were thought assuredly to be dead. They were technically classified as either killed in action (KIA) or presumed to have died at the time of their disappearance.

The U.S. government, though believing that most, if not all, of the additional personnel were dead, placed their names on the MIA/POW list for a specific reason. It was a political reason that greatly increased the chances of finding their remains—or the men themselves, if some were, miraculously, still alive. That reason will be discussed in the next chapter.

Air-Crash Victims

Several hundred of the personnel on the list were the victims of air crashes, among them the men who went down with the B-52 bomber and the AC-130 gunship in December 1972. These men make up much of the type that does not fit the usual meaning of "missing in action" because the government has a very definite idea of what became of them; it seems almost certain that no one survived such disasters.

Also included among the victims were 436 air force pilots who crashed at sea and were never found.[7] It seems just as certain that they, too, must have perished.

Although they do not fit the usual meaning given to "missing in action," it was appropriate to list all these crash victims as MIAs. This is because it only *seemed* certain that they were dead. There was no solid proof that they had died— and there would be no such proof until their bodies, or bits of their shattered bodies, were found and positively identified.

The same approach was taken with the airmen who plunged into the sea. Although they had never been found, there was no proof positive that they had died. And so they, too, could rightfully be counted as MIAs.

In some cases, there has always been the possibility, as remote as it might seem, that the crash victims survived and were taken prisoner. And always the possibility, again so very remote, that a few of the fliers who went into the sea were picked up by enemy ships or somehow managed to make their way to shore, there to be captured.

There is at least one instance on record of a pilot being captured after crashing at sea:

When his jet is hit while off the coast of North Vietnam, Air Force Capt. John Swanson parachutes into the water near several small boats. A fellow pilot observes the descent of his parachute. Swanson is not seen being taken aboard the boats, but U.S. intelligence officers later receive a report that he has been captured by North Vietnamese fishermen.[8]

The True MIAs

The cases of servicemen such as Sergeant Small and Captain Schmidt come closer to the way we have always thought of MIAs. They are the men who vanished after being taken prisoner or after being trapped in an area in which enemy troops were known to be nearby. Because they were definitely alive but never seen again, we have no idea of what happened to them and can only wonder about their fates.

Did those who were seen being taken prisoner die in captivity? Did the vanished Captain Schmidt and those who disappeared in battle die in dense jungle growth or high grass that kept their rescuers or comrades from seeing them? Or did some of their number survive and become prisoners? Are any of them still alive and being held captive after all these years?

And did some flee from battle with shattered nerves or desert the armed forces because they objected to the part being played by America in its most hated of all wars? Are they now living in Southeast Asia or elsewhere, afraid to come home or never wanting to see the United States again?

Questions. So many questions. And, as yet, no solid answers. Perhaps there will be no answers for years, or for all time, to come. These men are the truly missing in action.

HOW MANY MAY
STILL BE ALIVE?

This, too, is a question that is difficult, if not impossible, to answer. A possible answer, however, may be had by reading an article in a 1985 issue of the *New Republic* magazine.[9] The article's author, journalist James Rosenthal, says that it is possible that as many as 644 men are still alive. Here's how he figures things.

Of the more than 2,500 names on the expanded MIA/POW list, Rosenthal sets 2,477 as being actual MIAs. (This exact figure is presumably a total computed by the Department of Defense at the time.) He goes on to explain that almost half of the 2,477 MIAs, 1,186 in all, are men thought to have been killed in action but whose bodies have never been located. Next, he reports, the Department of Defense presumes that another 647 men were certainly killed because of the violence that accompanied their disappearances (air crashes, artillery barrages, and the such). In all, the number of those thought to have died stands at 1,833.

When those 1,833 are subtracted from 2,477, 644 men are left. Rosenthal writes that, in theory at least, they could still be alive somewhere in Southeast Asia.

But America's role in the war ended more than fifteen years ago. After so long a time, is it possible that any of those 644 men are still alive? Reports from Southeast Asia indicate that it may well be possible, if not probable, that they were still alive just recently. The reports are of MIAs being sighted. To cite just two examples:

In 1970, Army Specialist First Class James M. Rozo is taken prisoner while riding in a truck in South Vietnam. A year later, the army receives a report that Rozo has been seen as enemy troops are moving him in the direction of Cambodia. Another report comes through, fourteen years later, in 1985. It says that Rozo has escaped from captivity. At present, Rozo is thought to be living in Cambodia. His parents wonder if he is voluntarily remaining in Cambodia rather than coming home because he has started a family there.[10]

Air Force Col. David L. Hrdlicka's plane is shot down while over northern Laos on May 18, 1965. The next day, a China news agency broadcasts a report by Laotian communist forces that Hrdlicka has been captured. A year later, Laos broadcasts a letter that the colonel is said to have written; in it he talks of the war and his eagerness to see his family again. Next, in August 1967, the Russian newspaper *Pravda* publishes a photograph of Hrdlicka. It shows him under guard and wearing his flying suit. At the time, the United States suspects that he is being held captive in a cave in northern Laos. Reports believed to be about the colonel are received by American intelligence officers for a number of years. In 1986, twenty-one years after his disappearance, the Laotians pledge to supply information about Hrdlicka— but have not done so to date.[11]

As of this writing, there have been more than 7,150 alleged sightings of men thought to be MIAs in Vietnam, Laos, and Cambodia.[12] Many of the sightings were reported by Vietnamese refugees who have settled in the United States. The U.S. government claims that all the reports have been investigated and that all but a few have shown themselves to be without real merit. The government says that the remaining few are still being held open for further investigation. We'll talk of these reports in detail in a later chapter.

At present, though it is theoretically possible that 644 men are still alive, many people believe the total to be much lower. In 1981, *Time* magazine reported that the families of some MIAs were gauging the count to be around 300. A 1986 issue of the *New York Times* held that several U.S. government officials were estimating the total to be at least 100. In a recently published (1986) book, *Bitter Victory*, journalist Robert Shaplen writes that a substantial number of MIA families think that after the passage of so many years the living may have dwindled to a mere twelve or so, with some residing in Southeast Asia of their own accord, while others are being held captive.[13]

Despite these estimates, how many MIAs may actually still be alive? The answer, as always, remains unknown.

UNIQUE IN U.S. HISTORY

The widespread and continuing insistence that the Vietnam MIAs, alive and dead, be found is considered unique in American history. This is because only a few Americans were listed as missing in Vietnam in comparison to the number declared MIA in World War II and the Korean War. Yet, at the close of both those wars and in the years that followed, there was never an intense public demand that their MIAs be located and their fates determined.

Listed as missing in World War II were 78,751 men, while 8,177 went unaccounted for in the Korean conflict. The MIA total for World War II added up to just over 19 percent of the 405,399 Americans who died in the fighting. MIAs totaled approximately 15 percent of the 54,246 American fatalities in Korea. Vietnam's MIAs came to about 4 percent of the 55,582 U.S. troops killed.[14]

Why is it that, unlike the two preceding wars, there has been such an energetic call to learn the fate of the Vietnam MIAs? There seem to be several reasons. To begin with, both World War II and Korea, especially the former, were conflicts that most Americans supported. People, though mourning the dead, the maimed, and the missing, were resigned to think of them as the necessary though terrible costs of what were regarded as justifiable and even, particularly in the case of World War II, noble wars. Mourn as they did for the missing, they made no great demand that they be found.

The Vietnam War was another matter entirely. From its very start it was opposed by many Americans. Their ranks, swelled by protesters worldwide, grew through the years of fighting until the war became the most widely hated conflict in U.S. history. To worsen matters, it ended in defeat for the nation and spread a sense of humiliation across the land. Americans everywhere felt that their country had lost its honor. As James Rosenthal puts it in his *New Republic* article, the recovery of the MIAs, both the living and the dead, became—and remains—a matter connected with the restoration of the nation's honor. For years now, their return has been seen as symbolic of that honor being regained.[15]

Furthermore, in the aftermath of both World War II and Korea, the United States had access to the countries in which the men had been lost. Worried families knew that if their missing loved ones were still alive and being held captive, there was a good chance that they would be found. When the MIAs were not located, their families felt certain that they had died. The families could then get on with their lives.*

Again, Vietnam was another matter entirely. Soon after the American forces withdrew, the North Vietnamese asserted their control over the entire nation and, because of a series of postwar problems that will be discussed in the next chapter, closed it to the United States. Since then, they have allowed only a few U.S. diplomatic missions and MIA search parties to enter Vietnam. Political problems have likewise hampered MIA efforts in neighboring Laos and Cambodia,

---

*In recent years, perhaps due to public concern for the missing in Vietnam, the U.S. press has shown a growing interest in the fates of the World War II and Korean MIAs. Recent news reports indicate that the remains of some 390 Americans may still be in North Korea; in September 1986, the bodies of eleven servicemen were finally returned to U.S. hands, more than thirty years after the close of the Korean conflict. As for World War II, a 1986 report held that as late as nine years after the victory in Europe, the United States knew that its former ally, the Soviet Union, was holding more than 6,000 American personnel captive. U.S. efforts to secure their release constantly met with Soviet denials of any knowledge of them. No one knows how many of the men are yet alive in Russia and its satellite nations.[16]

Among the Americans concerned for the MIAs of these long-ago wars is Adrian Fisch. Fisch heads Red Badge of Courage (RBC), a Minnesota-based organization of citizens and veterans. The RBC was founded in 1970 and, as its letterhead states, works "For the Return of *All* MIAs/POWs."

both of which are strongly influenced by the Vietnamese. And so, millions of Americans are worried that an undetermined number of living and dead U.S. service personnel are still being held there. They want them found and brought home.

As we'll see in greater detail later on, there are various other reasons why the Vietnam MIA issue has remained at the forefront of so many American minds through the years. For one, the MIA families have loudly complained that for political reasons the U.S. government has not tried hard enough to recover both the living and dead MIAs. And, for another, there have been those many disquieting reports, more than 7,150 at the time this book is being written, of MIAs being sighted in various parts of Southeast Asia.

One more reason must be mentioned. For years, many Americans, angered or humiliated by their country's involvement in Vietnam, did not want to think of the war. But the 1980s have brought a nationwide renewal of interest in the conflict. That renewed interest can be seen in the enthusiastic reception given such motion pictures as *Platoon* and *Full Metal Jacket,* both released in 1987. Among the most popular of the Vietnam films have been those dealing with the MIAs and POWs: Sylvester Stallone's *Rambo,* Gene Hackman's *Uncommon Valor,* and Chuck Norris's *Missing in Action* series. They have stirred the imaginations of millions of Americans, have promoted the idea that there must be POWs and MIAs being held captive, and have heightened the feeling that it is a matter of heroism and national honor to locate and retrieve all the missing, whether living or dead.

And so the stage is set for the drama. The curtain now rises on the first of its many acts and takes us back to 1973.

Chapter Two
A TROUBLED
BEGINNING

The day was Tuesday, January 23, 1973. Halfway across the world from Vietnam, the French skies above the city of Paris were gray and wet with drizzle when U.S. presidential adviser Henry Kissinger met there with Le Duc Tho of the North Vietnamese Politburo. Together, at 12:45 P.M., they put their initials to a pact that was intended to bring peace to Vietnam and mark the end of U.S. participation in the war.[1]

FIVE TEMPESTUOUS YEARS

The scratch of their pens brought to a close a tempestuous period that dated back five years. Meeting in Paris in 1968, the United States and North Vietnam had begun a series of peace talks that were to be strained always by anger and suspicion on both sides. At the same time, President Richard M. Nixon had embarked along another course. He set out to end

America's involvement in the war through a policy that came to be known as Vietnamization.

It was a policy that called for the United States to build up the Army of South Vietnam (ARVN) to the point where, without outside support, it could defend itself against the North Vietnamese army and its guerrilla force in the south, the Vietcong. In keeping with the policy, Mr. Nixon had begun to remove U.S. troops from Southeast Asia in 1969. By 1971, the South Vietnamese had assumed the main responsibility for the ground fighting in their country. The United States had continued to provide them with air support and economic aid; the air support included heavy bombing strikes against the North Vietnamese.

Continuing to be marked by suspicion and anger—and damaged constantly by word of the intense fighting in Vietnam and the American air strikes—the Paris peace talks had struggled on until March 1972, when they finally collapsed. They were resumed at midyear, however. This time, in contrast to all that had gone before, they were successful. Now, at 12:45 P.M. on a wet Tuesday in January 1973, they came to a close with the Kissinger-Tho initialing of a pact known as the Agreement on Ending the War and Restoring Peace in Vietnam.[2]

The pact was formally signed four days later. Calling for a Vietnam cease-fire to begin at 2400 hours GMT (12 midnight, Greenwich mean time) on January 27, 1973, it was divided into nine sections, known as *chapters*. Those sections

Henry Kissinger (seated, background) and North Vietnamese Politburo member Le Duc Tho (seated, foreground) putting their initials to the Vietnam peace agreement. Kissinger, who later became Secretary of State, and Tho were awarded the 1973 Nobel Peace Prize for their efforts in bringing an end to the Vietnam War.

contained twenty-three separate agreements.[3] The agreements covered a wide range of matters. One, for example, stipulated that the United States would withdraw all its armed forces within sixty days. Another voiced the understanding that North and South Vietnam would be reunified as a single nation by peaceful means.

It was a pact that was doomed to failure. It saw the last of the U.S. forces withdrawn from Vietnam, but it did nothing to end the fighting there.

THE PACT: MIAs AND POWs

Of the pact's twenty-three agreements, two pertained directly to the MIAs and prisoners of war. They were:

> The return of captured military personnel and foreign civilians . . . shall be carried out simultaneously with and completed not later than the same day as the troop withdrawal. . . . *(Not only were American troops to be withdrawn but also the forces of other nations that had supported South Vietnam.)*

> The parties shall help each other to get information about those military personnel and foreign civilians of the parties missing in action, to determine the location and take care of the graves of the dead so as to facilitate the exhumation and repatriation of the remains.[4]

The wording of the second agreement explains why the U.S. government added to its initial list of 800 MIAs and POWs the names of the air-crash victims and other service personnel who were thought to be dead but whose bodies had never been found. By including their names on the list, the United States, through working with the North Vietnamese under the terms of the agreement, gave itself the best chance possible of learning what had become of the missing and of having both the living and dead returned home.

TROUBLE LOOMS

Work on the release of POWs began immediately and went smoothly at first. American and North Vietnamese prisoners were exchanged in the next weeks. The return of the American POWs was called Operation Homecoming and was completed by March 29, 1973. Returned to the United States were 591 prisoners.[5] But the exchange soon ran into trouble because both sides accused the other of not returning all their men. The Americans were to repeat the charge for years to come.

The work on the MIA provision took shape with the formation of a Four-Party Joint Military Team.[6] Its job was to discuss the living and dead missing and to facilitate an exchange of information that would lead to their being found. The team, which met twice a week (on Tuesdays and Thursdays) at Tansonnhut near Saigon, consisted of members from the United States, North Vietnam, South Vietnam, and the People's Revolutionary Government (PRG). The PRG, founded by communist factions in the south, was a government established in opposition to the South Vietnamese government.

As did the exchange of prisoners, the initial MIA work went smoothly. The Americans on the team were surprised at the cooperation shown by the northern members. The North Vietnamese began by saying that they looked on the return of the missing as a "humanitarian" issue meant to end the anguish and uncertainty suffered by so many U.S. families. They then voiced the desire never to see the MIA work damaged or hampered by any troubles that might arise out of the various cease-fire agreements. Finally, they reported that an effort was under way to collect information on missing U.S. ground and air personnel. In a matter of months they arranged for the return of the remains of twenty-three deceased Americans.

These words were soon backed with action. The northerners granted permission for U.S. search parties to visit known

Above: *members of the Four-Party Joint Military Team meet to coordinate the release of POWs in early 1973.* Facing page: *a former POW officer carries his six-year-old son, whom he had never seen before, and walks with his daughter and wife following his arrival home to the United States during Operation Homecoming. He had been captured by the North Vietnamese in 1967.*

air-crash sites in South Vietnam in the hope of finding the remains of the victims. As a result, eighteen searches were conducted between May and December 1973; found were the remains of nine missing Americans. Of that number, seven were discovered at a dense jungle location about 200 miles (340 km) northeast of Saigon. A helicopter, missing on a 1969 flight, had crashed there. The searchers were led to the spot by local hunters who had come upon the downed helicopter sometime earlier.

Though the MIA efforts began smoothly, they soon ran into trouble. It was trouble that stemmed from the very matters that the North Vietnamese members said should not hamper the MIA work—namely, any problems that might arise out of the cease-fire agreements. Those agreements were now proving to be more than troublesome. They were being violated, to one degree or another, by both the United States and North Vietnam. For example, here are just three of the agreements and a brief account of what was happening to each:

> The reunification of Vietnam shall be carried out step by step through peaceful means on the basis of discussions and agreements between North and South Vietnam, without coercion or annexation by either party.

In American eyes, the North Vietnamese were in total violation of this provision. They and their South Vietnamese allies, the Vietcong, were continuing to attack in the south, their aim being to take control of the capital city of Saigon. Reunification of the nation was completed in April 1975, but not by means of the agreement. It came when, after a long siege, Saigon fell to North Vietnamese and Vietcong troops. Formal reunification was completed by the North Vietnamese in July 1976, and the entire country was renamed the Socialist Republic of Vietnam.

> The South Vietnamese people shall decide themselves the political future of South Vietnam through genuinely

free and democratic elections under international supervision.

The Americans were quick to suspect that the North Vietnamese, attacking toward Saigon as they were, had no intention of allowing the South Vietnamese to decide the future of their country through "free and democratic elections." Those suspicions eventually proved themselves correct. The North Vietnamese never arranged for any sort of election after taking Saigon. They established the reunified Vietnam as a communist state, with Hanoi as its capital city.

The United States shall not continue its military involvement or intervene in the internal affairs of South Vietnam.

After withdrawing its troops, the United States did not continue its direct military involvement in South Vietnam. However, the United States insisted that the South Vietnam government at Saigon was the true Vietnamese government and continued to supply it with military goods and other aid. The North Vietnamese charged that, in doing so, America was turning its back on its agreement not to "intervene in the internal affairs of South Vietnam."

The various charges flew back and forth. Anger broke out on both sides of the fence and made any sort of U.S.–North Vietnamese cooperation under the cease-fire pact increasingly difficult and, at last, impossible. The anger filtered down to members of the Four-Party Joint Military Team, and their MIA work together began to disintegrate.

A December Tragedy
That disintegration led to a tragedy for the Americans on December 15, 1973, when three helicopters landed at a spot about 10 miles (17 km) southwest of Saigon. Their job was to unload a U.S. team that planned to investigate a nearby air-crash site.[7]

The helicopters, with South Vietnamese pilots at the controls, were unarmed and marked with the orange stripes that identified them as being involved in cease-fire work. The search team itself was also unarmed.

As the team members were disembarking, however, gunfire and rocket grenades burst from the surrounding foliage. One of the helicopters took a direct grenade hit. The helicopter exploded in flames, and its pilot was killed instantly. There was a sudden roar of engines as the remaining two helicopters took to the air and escaped to safety.

The team members, who had thrown themselves flat on the ground, were left stranded. One of their number, Capt. Richard M. Rees, came to his feet and held his arms above his head. It could be clearly seen that he carried no weapons and that, like his fellow team members, he wore an orange armband. He yelled in the direction of the foliage, perhaps shouting that he and his men were unarmed and on official cease-fire business. His companions had no idea what he was saying; they could not hear him above the gunfire and exploding rockets.

As Rees stood there with his arms upraised, the gunfire continued. Suddenly, he toppled over backward. The men closest by crawled to him. They found him dead.

The captain's death enraged the Americans on the Joint Military Team. Saying that he had been murdered in cold blood, they told the North Vietnamese that they had always asked for permission to dispatch search teams and had done so in this case, receiving the necessary clearance before sending the three helicopters out. The northerners should have made sure that no harm befell the team in an area that proved to be unsafe because of the fighting still going on there between the North and South Vietnamese.

They added that team members from the PRG had once warned them to stay clear of another search area because it was thought unsafe. Since that sort of information had been given voluntarily, the Americans said that they had expected the PRG members to do the same thing in all future instances. Such a caution should have been forthcoming in the case of the Rees team. Why had it been withheld?

The North Vietnamese replied that a warning had not been issued because they and the PRG members had no idea that the Rees team planned a search. They insisted that no request for permission to investigate the area southwest of Saigon had been received from the Americans.

The Americans looked upon the reply as an outright lie. As a consequence of the captain's death and the angry exchange of words, U.S. investigations of crash sites were halted for years to come.

OTHER PROBLEMS

Violations of the cease-fire pact were not the only problems that filtered down to damage the MIA work during 1973. There were two other developments of extreme importance.

The first had to do with the fact that the Vietnam War had early spread to neighboring Laos and Cambodia. The fighting there had first taken shape when U.S. and South Vietnamese troops attacked North Vietnamese troops that were using the two nations as refuges and training grounds. Though both countries were the scenes of much bloodshed, the cease-fire pact contained no detailed mention of how peace would be restored to them.

And so, as in Vietnam itself, the Laotian and Cambodian fighting continued. Local communist forces—the Pathet Lao in Laos and the Khmer Rouge in Cambodia—went on battling to overthrow two governments toward which the United States was sympathetic. Both of the communist forces were backed and armed by the North Vietnamese, and both were resisted by the Americans, who subjected them to air bombings. This resulted in United States–North Vietnamese relations worsening still further as the months passed.[8]

The second problem was an economic one. It caused the Americans on the Joint Military Team to say that their MIA work was being made the subject of economic blackmail.

ECONOMIC BLACKMAIL

One of the cease-fire agreements called for the United States to provide the North Vietnamese with postwar economic aid. The provision stated:

> In pursuance of its traditional policy, the United States will contribute to healing the wounds of war and to postwar reconstruction of the Democratic Republic of Vietnam and throughout Indochina.

No specific dollar amount for the aid was mentioned in the pact. However, a few days after the pact had been signed, President Nixon sent a letter to North Vietnam's prime minister, Pham Van Dong. Mr. Nixon wrote that he thought the amount should run to about $3.25 billion over a five-year period. Because of the letter, a joint U.S.–North Vietnamese commission was immediately established to work out the details of a plan under which the assistance would be given.

The funds, however, could not be awarded without the approval of the U.S. Congress. This fact was pressed home to the North Vietnamese by presidential adviser Henry Kissinger. But they paid little heed to Kissinger's warning; they looked upon the Nixon letter as containing a binding promise to provide them with aid amounting to at least $3.25 billion.

Consequently, the North Vietnamese thought themselves being cheated when Mr. Nixon began to place limitations on the award of the funds. Specifically, he tied the award to two matters: (1) the slowing of work on the MIA/POW issue because of the pact violations and (2) the fighting in Laos and Cambodia. The president said that the aid would not be given until there was better progress on the MIA/POW problem and until definite steps were taken to stop the fighting in Laos and Cambodia.[9]*

---

*In the end, the aid was never given. And, in the end, the Laotian government fell to the political faction known as the Pathet Lao. The fall came in 1975, with Laos then taking a new name, the Lao People's Democratic Republic,

By late 1973 the fresh anger generated by Mr. Nixon's revised position on economic aid was affecting the Joint Military Team. The early cooperation shown by the North Vietnamese members evaporated. Increasingly, they refused or simply ignored any U.S. requests for permission to visit aircrash sites. Their efforts to inform the American members of living and dead MIAs diminished. Despite their early statements that the MIA work was a "humanitarian" issue that must not be influenced by difficulties with the cease-fire pact, they now said that it must be related to other matters—specifically, the question of the $3.25 billion in promised U.S. aid.[10]

The Americans responded angrily to these tactics. They charged that the progress on locating and retrieving the MIAs was being stalled by what they called "economic blackmail."

In his book *Without Honor*, journalist Arnold R. Isaacs writes that the American charge here was a valid one. As proof, he quotes a remark made by a North Vietnamese member of the Joint Military Team to an American member during a break in one of the team's meetings. The North Vietnamese officer said that his country *did* have information on many American MIAs. In some instances, Vietnam held the remains of downed pilots. He added that Vietnam did not like having these men and that their graves were not only insults to his homeland's soil but awful reminders of what the U.S. Air Force bombings had done.

The speaker went on to say that Vietnam wanted to return the MIAs to American hands. But, he asked, why should they be handed over for nothing? The U.S. government had

and coming under strong Vietnamese influence. As for Cambodia, it has been torn by strife ever since the Vietnam War. Its present government was established in 1979 with the help of Vietnamese troops. Throughout the 1980s, it has battled with the heavily-armed forces of an opposition movement.

The Cambodian fighting and Vietnam's desire for financial aid from the United States have both played a part in the MIA drama for years now and are continuing to play a role as this book is being written.

done much harm to Vietnam and its people and must pay for the damage. Even President Nixon recognized this as fact and had committed himself to the payment of reparations. And so, the North Vietnamese member concluded, Vietnam saw no reason to surrender the men just because the United States wanted them back and was demanding their return.[11]

Because of the pact violations, the fighting, the North Vietnamese accusations of a promise broken by President Nixon, and the U.S. charges of economic blackmail, the work of finding and retrieving the MIAs lay in ruins by the close of 1973. The searches for crash sites came to an end. The Joint Military Team struggled on until it was disbanded in 1974.[12]

But the MIA drama was still just at its beginning; it would see many developments in the next fifteen years. Among the first of these developments was a complex of reports, doubts, suspicions, and strange happenings that had to do with Americans thought to be alive and held captive in Southeast Asia.

Chapter Three
THE LIVING: Doubts
and Suspicions

The doubts and suspicions first showed themselves in late March 1973, as soon as the North Vietnamese released 591 American prisoners of war in Operation Homecoming. U.S. officials on the scene immediately complained that this number could not possibly represent all the men held captive by the enemy. There were two reasons for their complaints.

TWO COMPLAINTS

First, the Defense Department's expanded list of MIAs and POWs contained *over 2,500* names. Surely, more than just 591 men should have been returned.

Second, as *National Review* magazine noted in 1981, not one of the 591 returning men was maimed or seriously injured. Certainly some of their number—men who had been taken in battle or had escaped from flaming or exploding aircraft—should have been scarred or should have been missing an arm, a leg, or an eye.[1] To U.S. minds, this could mean just one thing: The North Vietnamese were withholding those captives who had survived a terrible injury or who bore the marks of prison camp rigors. They were holding them back because they were afraid of being accused of mistreatment or improper care.

The North Vietnamese replied to these charges by insisting that they held no other U.S. personnel in captivity. But American officials, their suspicions unallayed, continued to demand that any unreleased POWs be handed over immediately. The North Vietnamese went on saying that all prisoners had been accounted for. Both sides held to their positions throughout 1973 and 1974. Meanwhile, U.S.–North Vietnamese relations steadily deteriorated due to violations of the cease-fire pact and the animosities created by President Nixon's changed attitude on his proffered economic aid.

The feelings of U.S. officials on the scene were shared by the MIA families back home. Then, because of a step taken by the government in Washington in 1975, a new kind of doubt and suspicion spread throughout the nation. It was a doubt and suspicion directed not at the North Vietnamese but at Washington itself.

A CONGRESSIONAL STUDY

By 1975, a new president, Gerald R. Ford, was in the White House following President Nixon's resignation due to matters unrelated to the MIA/POW issue. Disturbed over the nagging issue, President Ford appointed a group of ten congressional members to study the MIA/POW problem. In September that year the House Select Committee on Missing Persons in Southeast Asia was formed.[2]

Under the chairmanship of Rep. G. V. "Sonny" Montgomery of Mississippi, the committee spent fifteen months at its work. It reviewed the files on 200 missing personnel, studied 100 other documents pertaining to the MIAs and POWs, and interviewed 50 of the nation's leading government figures. Among those interviewed were President Ford himself, former Secretary of Defense Donald Rumsfeld, and Henry Kissinger. Kissinger by now had advanced from presidential adviser to secretary of state. (He took the post in 1973 and held it until 1977.)

Montgomery and his fellow committee members also traveled to Hanoi to speak with some of the North Vietnamese leaders. There the members were given the now long-standing assurance that no American servicemen were still being held in captivity.

The committee members worked until the autumn of 1976. Then, in mid-December, Chairman Montgomery presented a report on the outcome of their investigation. He told a battery of television cameras that the committee—on the basis of its studies, its interviews with fifty of the nation's leaders, and its visit to North Vietnam—had found that "no Americans are being held alive as prisoners in Indochina, or elsewhere, as a result of the war in Indochina." To this, the report added: "The sad conclusion is that there is no evidence that . . . missing Americans are still alive."

AN ANGRY REACTION

Montgomery's presentation was met with anger and doubt by MIA families everywhere and was called *his* version of the committee's findings rather than a true report of what the committee believed. Certain of the nation's ranking officials and great segments of the public joined the families in their skepticism. The widespread belief was that Montgomery, backed only by certain of the committee members, had not told the truth about the MIAs and POWs. (We'll see later that fully half the committee membership did disagree with the chairman's announcement.) He and his supporters were accused of cooperating with the government's desire to be rid of the entire issue.

But why should anyone suspect the government of wishing to be rid of the MIA/POW issue? The critics of the committee gave two answers: First, they charged that Washington wanted to "close the books" on the matter as part of putting a hated war quickly into the past and ending the terrible divisions that America's participation in it had caused among the people. A continuing quest for the MIAs and POWs would keep a festering memory from healing over.

Second, they argued that Washington, while having no desire to pay former President Nixon's proffered $3.25 billion in aid, was nevertheless seeking to establish good relations and diplomatic ties with the new Vietnamese government. Politically, it was doing so in the hope of restoring stability in Southeast Asia. Economically, it was hoping to take advantage of certain benefits available in Vietnam—particularly the rich oil deposits thought to lie off its coast.[3] Heated negotiations for the return of the MIAs and POWs could damage these efforts. As the committee critics saw things, the ugly truth was that Washington was willing to exchange the lives of its lost servicemen for political and economic gains.

The committee report was also greeted with doubt for other reasons. As we'll soon discuss in detail, reports of living Americans being sighted in Southeast Asia were being received in the United States. In light of those reports, a great many people simply could not believe that not a single American was still alive and being held captive in Vietnam and its neighbors, Laos and Cambodia, or living voluntarily in any of the three countries. Among the doubters were two high-

Chairman G. V. "Sonny" Montgomery caused an angry reaction when he stated there were no living MIAs or POWs in Southeast Asia. His committee's findings were met with widespread skepticism.

ranking military figures: Gen. William C. Westmoreland and Adm. John C. McCain.

General Westmoreland commanded the U.S. forces in Vietnam from 1963 to 1968. In 1987, *Life* magazine reported that he felt the North Vietnamese had always played "word games" in the POW issue. The general pointed out that they had invariably said that no Americans were being held captive *in Vietnam*. They had, so far as he knew, never mentioned Laos or Cambodia. Five hundred and fifty-six U.S. personnel, you'll remember, had disappeared in Laos, and in Cambodia eighty-two had disappeared. Westmoreland contended that the North Vietnamese, by not mentioning these two countries, were deliberately ignoring the fates of more than 630 lost Americans.[4]

Adm. John C. McCain* served as the commander in chief of the Pacific forces from 1968 to 1972. In 1976, he told Congress that the North Vietnamese had deceived the United States when they claimed to have no information on the MIAs and POWs. He felt there was no question that some of the country's missing men were still alive in Southeast Asia.[5]

THE HARSHEST CRITICISM

Some of the harshest criticism of the committee report came from the National League of Families of American Prisoners and Missing in Southeast Asia (NLF), one of the several citizen organizations that were formed in the 1970s to urge the quest for the MIAs and POWs. Among such groups were Red Badge of Courage (founded in 1970), Forgotten Americans Need Support (1971), and the National Human Rights Committee for POW/MIAs (1977). Joining their ranks later

---

*Admiral McCain died some years ago. His son, Navy Lt. Comdr. John McCain, was shot down while flying above Hanoi in 1968, was held captive for five years, and suffered torture during that time. Mr. McCain is now a member of the U.S. Senate. He represents Arizona.

were Seaside Support League—POW/MIA (1980) and the National Vietnam Veterans Coalition (1984).

Formed in 1970, the NLF was dedicated to learning the status of all missing servicemen, to helping bring home both the dead and the living, and to distributing information on the MIA/POW issue to the MIA families and the general public. The NLF continues its work today. Made up of concerned Americans and the families and friends of the missing, it has a membership of more than 3,400 and is divided into five regional and fifty local groups.[6]

The organization attacked the report along several fronts. For example, the NFL claimed that its leadership had asked to be allowed to be in close contact with the committee and to provide it with information; the request had been refused. Furthermore, the NLF had been troubled by the size of the staff being formed to help the committee and had called it too small; this concern had gone ignored by the committee. Moreover, the league charged the committee with holding most of its meetings behind closed doors, with the result that the NLF was never privy to what was being discussed and learned.

The league went on to say that during the committee's Hanoi visit the North Vietnamese had lied about holding no U.S. captives and that Chairman Montgomery had swallowed this lie. That the North Vietnamese were indeed lying is borne out by 1979 and 1981 reports in *National Review*.[7]

In both issues, the *Review* stated that at the time of the Hanoi visit the United States was in possession of information concerning a missing civilian: a retired Central Intelligence Agency (CIA) official named Tucker Gougglemann. The information held that Gougglemann was imprisoned in Vietnam. When the committee members asked about him, the Vietnamese denied holding the man. Yet, a year later, they turned over Gougglemann's remains to another U.S. delegation and said that he had died in prison in June 1975— fully six months before the committee visit.

The United States had also heard of another imprisoned

American civilian: a man named Arlow Gay. Again, when questioned by the committee, the North Vietnamese shook their heads. Sometime later, Gay was released from captivity.

But is it possible that the North Vietnamese leaders were telling the truth—possible that they actually did not know the two men were imprisoned in their country at the time of the committee visit and did not learn of their presence until later? It hardly seems likely. Had Gougglemann and Gay been servicemen, they would have been just two of many and might have been somehow overlooked. But both were civilians and thus more easily noticed. Furthermore, Gougglemann was a former CIA official.

Perhaps the NLF's most severe criticism was leveled at the committee's claim to have worked fifteen months on the MIA/POW issue. The league pointed out that the committee spent three months assembling its staff, finding a place to do its work, and beginning to put its files together. Then, so the league charged, the committee had actually devoted no more than six months to the study, with the members spending the rest of the time on vacations and political campaigns. The committee had simply spent too little time at its work to produce a report that the nation could accept as valid and competently done. In total, as the NLF judged the matter, the report was too hastily prepared and was the result of incomplete information from government sources.

TROUBLE WITHIN
THE COMMITTEE

Outsiders were not the only ones who disliked the report. Criticism also came from within the committee itself—in fact, as already mentioned, half its membership, five congressmen in all, was critical of the report. Led by Rep. Ben Gilman of New York, they said that the search for the POWs and MIAs should be continued. They based their remarks on findings they themselves had made over the months as part of their committee work. These findings, all indicating good reasons for *not* "closing the books" on the MIA/POW issue, were forwarded to the White House.

The findings of the five committeemen were received by a new president, Jimmy Carter, who had won the office in the 1976 election. Mr. Carter chose to ignore them in favor of the Montgomery report. Agreeing that there were no living U.S. captives yet in Vietnam, he said that the government would now concentrate its efforts on locating and retrieving the remains of dead MIAs.[8]

Mr. Carter's decision unleashed another storm of criticism from many people. If not "closing the books" on the entire MIA/POW issue, they said, the president was certainly trying to end any further work on behalf of prisoners still living. They felt it to be a work that the U.S. government would view as especially dangerous to the efforts to restore good relations with the new Vietnamese government. Accusations that the Vietnamese were heartlessly keeping Americans in captivity long after the war had ended would likely insult and antagonize the former enemy. It would be far safer to ask for the dead.

The criticism here was joined by a fear. Washington was receiving reports of missing Americans being sighted in Southeast Asia. Also, other MIA/POW information was arriving from various intelligence-gathering sources. There was the uneasy feeling that Washington would eventually turn its back on all such material because the government would *actually not want to find* any of the MIAs and POWs who were still living. Their discovery would be embarrassing and humiliating to a government that had so firmly insisted that not one of their number was still alive.

There was another side to this fear. Many Americans began to suspect that their government, in its hope to avoid embarrassment and its desire for improved relations with the Vietnamese, was engaged in a "cover-up" conspiracy to keep the nation in the dark about the true status of the MIAs and POWs, both living and dead, and about the information concerning them. It is a suspicion that has persisted to this day.[9]*

And so the House Select Committee's report, as announced by Rep. "Sonny" Montgomery, unleashed a variety of fears and suspicions about how honestly and competently the MIA/POW problem was being handled. The report continues to be widely doubted and scorned today; these outlooks have stained the MIA/POW issue for years. The reasons why the report has remained so doubted and scorned are based on the fact that those passing years have witnessed an ever increasing number of disturbing reports from Southeast Asia—reports of American servicemen being sighted there.

---

*During the Carter years, two actions were taken that greatly strengthened the suspicion of a cover-up. First, in 1978, the Department of Defense declared all the missing men to be "presumed dead." The department announced that it was taking this step so that the MIA families could receive the financial benefits due them for a deceased relative. Many of the families saw the step as one more cover-up strategy. By declaring the men "presumed dead," they charged, the government was trying to help the nation forget them. Only one man, Air Force Col. Charles E. Shelton, has remained listed as a POW. He is listed as a symbol of the missing.[10]

Second, in 1980, Mr. Carter called for much of the information that had been received on the POWs and MIAs over the years to be designated as "classified" by the government. This meant that the information would no longer be available for inspection by the public and press. Hitherto, it had been designated as "unclassified" and had been open to everyone. The Carter administration said that the material was being reclassified because it contained much secret intelligence information that could be of value to the Vietnamese if it fell into their hands and much information that, if known to the former enemy, could place the eventual return of the MIAs in jeopardy.[11] Many people felt that the government was trying to keep everyone in the dark about the MIAs. They saw it as yet another strategy for inducing public forgetfulness and hastening the "closing of the books" on the issue.

Chapter Four
THE LIVING:
Were They Seen?

The reports of living American servicemen being sighted in Southeast Asia date back to 1975, the very year that saw the war end with the North Vietnamese capture of South Vietnam's capital city, Saigon. By 1983, word of 486 sightings had reached the United States. The number jumped to 3,508 by 1985. At the time this book is being written, the total stands at 7,156.[1]

WHY THE GROWING NUMBER?

What accounts for the continuing rise in sightings over the years? The answer is that since 1976 word of them has come mostly from the many refugees who have fled Vietnam, Cambodia, and Laos.

Though the war ended in 1975, the subsequent years were so filled with troubles for the three countries that a mass exodus over their borders resulted. When Saigon fell, thousands of people who had supported the South Vietnamese government or had served in its armed forces took flight to avoid being persecuted by the victorious northerners. Political and military strife plagued Laos and Cambodia, driving countless of their citizens to flight. Many of the refugees made their way to nearby Thailand, where camps were set up to house them while they waited to return home when peace was restored or to emigrate to a foreign country, hopefully the United States.

From Laos

A great many of the sightings were reported by Laotians while they were in the Thai refugee camps or after they had arrived in the United States. They claimed to have seen American captives either held under guard or penned in jungle compounds and caves back home.

One refugee, a Laotian pilot who made his way out of Southeast Asia in 1980, reported that he had spent eighteen years in a communist prison camp. He claimed to have had a number of Americans as cellmates during that time and reported that seven had died while in captivity. He estimated that between forty and fifty Americans were still being held prisoner in Laos seven years after the United States had withdrawn from the fighting.[2]

From Vietnam

From Vietnam itself came the report of a woman refugee. She told U.S. authorities that she had seen four Americans near Saigon in 1977; they had been working in a field about 20 miles (34 km) outside the city. A Vietnamese doctor was responsible for a later report. He claimed to have once treated a number of hospitalized American prisoners.[3]

A young Vietnamese refugee
waits for a new home.

Still another report from Vietnam was made by a former lieutenant in the South Vietnamese army. He claimed to have spent 1975 in an enemy prison camp. While there, he met several American inmates who were being held in a compound separate from the South Vietnamese captives. The lieutenant got to know them when he was assigned the job of bringing them their meals. He said that they were forced to build roads and were kept with their hands and legs tied when not working. Their senior officer was an army major who had been captured in 1971. Others in the group included a first lieutenant and two sergeants.[4]

From an American

One report of sightings inside Vietnam was made by an American: Marine Pfc. Robert Garwood. He mysteriously disappeared from his unit in 1965 and did not reappear until 1979. On his return home, Garwood said that he had spent the intervening fourteen years in North Vietnam. He claimed that in the late 1970s there were Americans being held in four prison camps there. Two were located on the edge of the city of Hanoi, and the remaining two lay in the countryside some 40 miles (68 km) to the northwest.

Garwood, when questioned on the number of prisoners at the camps, said that he had seen between forty and sixty each at two of the sites. The other two camps had each held about six or seven men. Then he said that during 1977 he had worked as a truck mechanic at Yen Bai, which lies about 80 miles (136 km) northwest of Hanoi. While there, he had watched a train of freight cars brake to a stop. Out of them came a number of South Vietnamese prisoners and between thirty and forty Caucasian men who spoke American English. Garwood described the Caucasians as clean shaven and wearing khaki work clothes. He added that they were healthy enough to have gotten down from the boxcars and then to have climbed back aboard them when the time came for the train to depart.[5]

THE SIGHTINGS:
TRUE OR FALSE?

Speaking as they do of Americans long held in captivity, the reported sightings are deeply troubling. But for years they have met with as much doubt on their side of the fence as the House Select Committee's report has on its side. A serious question has always surrounded them: Can they be accepted as truth?

The answer seems to be that some can be trusted. In the eyes of many U.S. officials, however, the majority must be treated with doubt. The officials list several reasons for their skepticism.

To begin, there is the fact that so many of the reports have come from refugees who have settled in the United States. Most of these people have arrived with little more than the clothes on their backs. Consequently, a spokesman for the Department of Defense, Col. Howard Hill,* voices a widespread official suspicion when he states his belief that many refugees have fabricated reports of sightings in the hope that the U.S. government would show its appreciation by helping them as they started life in their new country.[7]

Other officials point to the refugee camps in Thailand. Because the camps are filled with people yearning to emigrate to the United States, there is the belief that many of their number make up stories of sightings in the hope that an appreciative American government will give them better food and extra blankets while in the camps and then help them gain entry to the United States.[8]

Other Doubts

There are still more reasons for the official doubts. For one, many of the reports are regarded as too indefinite in their

---

*Colonel Hill was himself a Vietnam POW. He was held captive at the notorious Hanoi prison known to its inmates as the "Hanoi Hilton."[6]

descriptions of the sighted personnel to be taken seriously. Some descriptions, for example, are of men who could be from any of several countries but have been reported as Americans simply because they were not Asians. Others are of men who seemed to be under guard; when questioned at length, some of the refugees reporting them have admitted that they could not be certain that the men were actually being guarded. The men may have been Europeans. Or the refugees may have seen one or more of the American ex-servicemen (their number is unknown) who are thought to be living in Southeast Asia of their own free will.

Furthermore, many of the reports have not been of first-hand sightings. Rather, they have been reports from refugees who only heard about prisoners being sighted. They are discounted as being hearsay and are considered practically worthless.

Finally, there are doubts concerning specific sightings. Take, for example, the report of the woman refugee who said she had seen four Americans working in a field near Saigon in 1977. Officials view her report with suspicion because that field is known to border a major highway. They believe that Vietnam's communist government would not, while denying that it holds any U.S. prisoners, place four Americans in a spot where they could so easily be seen by visitors and delegations from foreign nations.[9]

The Garwood Report

And what of the report by Marine Pfc. Robert Garwood? It has long been questioned due to the circumstances surrounding his case. On at least three counts, he was thought to have been a deserter or a POW who had collaborated with the enemy. First, he had mysteriously disappeared from his unit. Second, there had been reports of his activities through the years—reports that he had led Vietcong troops against U.S. forces, that he had physically and verbally abused American prisoners, and that he had shouted communist propaganda at them through a bullhorn. Finally, on Garwood's return home, the North Vietnamese announced that he had lived among them of his own accord.

The marine corps placed Garwood on trial. In the end, the corps judged him innocent of desertion but guilty of collaborating with the enemy. Throughout his trial, Garwood did not speak of his North Vietnam sightings. He maintained his silence until the 1980s.[10]

The circumstances surrounding Garwood's case were not alone in creating official doubts about his sightings. It was also felt that the man, who disappeared at age nineteen and returned a thin and balding thirty-three-year-old, was psychologically too unstable to be trusted.

Not everyone, however, has doubted Garwood, and two points must be kept in mind about his reports. First, when describing one of the prisons in Hanoi, he said that he had seen several American prisoners gathered near a cistern in a courtyard there. His description of the courtyard and the cistern matched that given of the prison by an Asian refugee. Then, in the 1980s, several U.S. congressmen were granted permission to visit Hanoi. They managed to enter the prison, where they saw the courtyard and the cistern. They returned home with the belief that Garwood had been speaking the truth.[11]

Second, the air force's Lt. Gen. Eugene Tighe, on hearing Garwood's reports, remarked that they did not sound "unrealistic." General Tighe said that some of Garwood's information dovetailed with data that he himself held. Until 1981, Tighe was director of the Defense Intelligence Agency (DIA), which is a branch of the Department of Defense. That agency was, and still is, responsible for receiving and evaluating all reported sightings of MIAs in Southeast Asia.[12]

THE SIGHTINGS: HOW MANY ARE TRUE?

In the face of so many official doubts, just how many of the sightings can be said to be of genuine worth? No one can answer for certain. All that we can do is try to get some idea of an answer by looking at how the DIA evaluates reported sightings and at what it has done over the years.

Much of the DIA's work centers on its computers, where data on all received reports and other information are stored. The data include known air-crash sites. More than 700 sites have been pinpointed to date.[13]

Also stored are the names and backgrounds of missing personnel whose fates have been pretty well established over the years. Chief among them are the airmen whose downed planes ended up in known crash sites. The DIA assumes that these victims, unless they were seen parachuting to safety, must have perished in the crashes. Listed in addition are the few living men who have emerged from Southeast Asia of their own accord in recent years. They include Robert Garwood and several ministers who remained as long as they could in Southeast Asia to serve their flocks.

Finally, the computers have information on satellite and aerial photographs of installations that seem to be prisons of some sort. They are thought likely to house Asian inmates but are kept on record on the chance that they might fit the locales given in any future reported sightings.

The word of any newly reported sighting is fed into the computers to ascertain if it can be connected to the stored data in any of several ways. It may, for example, match a previous sighting known to have been false. Or the description given of a sighted MIA may fit that of a missing serviceman whose death has already been determined.

The DIA also interviews the individuals making the reports. A matter of prime interest here is whether any report must be seriously doubted or discarded because it is not of a firsthand sighting. Some 994 of the 7,156 sightings reported by 1987 have been classed as firsthand sightings.

Finally, in an effort to expose false reports, the DIA asks the individuals to take polygraph (lie detector) tests. The tests are given only if the people agree to sit for them.

More of our answer may come to light when we look at

several examples of what the agency has done over the years. We'll begin with the 484 sightings reported by 1983. As *Newsweek* magazine reported that year, the DIA resolved 268 of their number—meaning that it had been able to connect with them servicemen already well established as dead. About 3 percent of the 268 reports were found to be fictitious— either imagined by a refugee or invented in the hope that the story of the sighting would bring special treatment by the government. Left unresolved of the 484 sightings were 216. They were being kept open for further investigation in the hope they might one day produce concrete leads to one or more missing men.[14]

Next, let's move to the 3,508 sightings that were on record by 1985. James Rosenthal, writing in the *New Republic,* reports that only 751 were by people who said they had seen the MIAs firsthand. The DIA resolved 77 percent of these claimed firsthand sightings in two ways. It either exposed them as fakes or linked them with missing personnel whose fates had been previously determined. Of the 3,508 sightings, the DIA discounted all but five as real possibilities for further investigation.

Rosenthal goes on to explain that the DIA gave polygraph tests to about forty people responsible for what were thought to be the most credible sightings between 1979 and 1985. The tests indicated that thirteen of the people showed no deception in their stories. Two tests proved to be inconclusive, and twenty-four people tested showed deception in their stories.

Of the thirteen people who revealed no deception, the agency found that four made reports of MIAs whose fates had previously been learned. Three gave reports that eventually proved to be sightings of men who were not prisoners. One report was finally exposed as a fabrication.[15]

Finally, we turn to the 994 firsthand sightings that had been received by 1987. The agency has resolved 872 of their number. Of those resolved cases, 213 have been found to be false, while 659 have been determined to involve MIAs whose fates earlier became known to the DIA. Left are 122 sightings that are as yet unresolved. They are still open for further investigation.[16]

The 122 unresolved cases can be divided into two categories. They are:

- Seventy-four cases dealing with Americans reportedly being held as prisoners.

- Forty-eight cases dealing with Caucasians who might have been Americans and might not have been prisoners.

The seventy-four cases concerning Americans reported as prisoners can then be divided as follows:

- Sixty-five cases that are considered "active." They offer the best chance for further information and investigation.

- Seven cases in which the information received in the reported sightings is too vague to be considered useful.

- Two cases in which the persons who reported the sightings can no longer be found.

And so, according to these various reports, the agency has resolved the great majority of sightings by pinpointing some to men whose fates are considered known, by dismissing others as unreliable because they are not of firsthand glimpses, and by exposing and discarding yet others as made-up. And what of the remaining sightings, the ones that have not been resolved and remain open for further investigation? In late 1987, *Life* magazine reported that of the 7,156 sightings on record to date, the U.S. government finds some seventy cases "most compelling"—meaning that they contain certain points of evidence that indicate the North Vietnamese know more about the men involved than they have thus far admitted.[17] The magazine was referring in round figures to the sixty-five to seventy-four "prisoner" cases mentioned above.

THE DIA:
SOME CRITICISMS

In common with so many of the reported sightings themselves, the DIA has been faced with much public and official suspicion over the years. Its work and the results it has achieved are criticized for several reasons. For one, many people do not trust its high rate of "resolving" cases, saying that the rate shows that the agency is really cooperating in what they see as the government's continuing effort to "close the books" on the MIA problem or cover it up. Others, while not necessarily agreeing with this view, say that the agency follows a set of unwise policies in its investigation of reported sightings.

A major criticism of DIA policy holds that the agency is loathe to trust the refugee reports by themselves and seems to share a belief long held by intelligence agencies everywhere—that people can and will tell lies. Before taking any report seriously, the agency wants to see it supported by what it calls "technical means." For example, suppose that there is a report of Americans being held in a prison compound. The agency will treat the sighting with skepticism unless it can be backed up by such "technical means," or evidence, as satellite and aerial photographs of the place. Furthermore, when considering the report of one refugee, the agency hesitates to take it seriously unless it is supported by one or more similar reports.[18]

In all, there is the feeling that the DIA's policies prompt it to turn away too quickly from the reported sightings. That quickness keeps the agency from pursuing many reports that might, in the end, yield solid information on a living American still in Southeast Asia.

Nevertheless, regardless of whether the DIA is following unwise policies or being prudently cautious in judging the reports, the question of how many living Americans are still in Southeast Asia remains a mystery. Though the agency has resolved the great bulk of the reports, we must remember that sixty-five to seventy-four cases are considered, in *Life* magazine's words, "most compelling" and are still being held open for further investigation. Perhaps they will one day show us the answer to the question that has disturbed the MIA families and millions of other Americans for years.

Chapter Five
THE LIVING:
Three Clues

For many Americans, the reported sightings are not the only indications that living U.S. personnel are still to be found in Southeast Asia. There are three other clues that point to the Vietnamese as being guilty not only of holding living POWs but also of concealing information about them and about any servicemen who, as seems to have been the case with Robert Garwood, are living among the former enemy of their own free will.

CLUE #1:
NORTH VIETNAMESE LIES

There can be little or no doubt that the North Vietnamese have lied about certain prisoners on a number of occasions. Prime examples here are the cases of Tucker Gougglemann and Arlow Gay, which were mentioned in chapter 3. As you'll recall, the House Select Committee, on asking about the two men during the 1975 visit to Hanoi, received the answer that the North Vietnamese knew nothing about them. The North Vietnamese then later released Gougglemann's remains and freed Gay from captivity.

The Gougglemann and Gay stories do not stand alone as indictments of North Vietnamese lies. There is also the case of Navy Lt. Ron Dodge:

When his plane is shot down over North Vietnam in 1967, Lieutenant Dodge ejects and lands safely by parachute. Moments later, he radios a fellow pilot that he can see the enemy approaching and is about to destroy his radio equipment. Before day's end, the North Vietnamese broadcast the news of Dodge's capture. A photograph of the flier—with his face dirt streaked and bruised and his head in bandages—is then released and printed in the French publication *Paris Match*. The North Vietnamese later feature Dodge in a propaganda film entitled *Pilots in Pajamas*. The word *Pajamas* refers to the look of the prison garb the captives were made to wear. Yet, whenever asked about him, the North Vietnamese deny any knowledge of Dodge. Then, topping off the lie, they return the flier's remains to U.S. hands in 1981. Returned with him are the bodies of two air force pilots. The North Vietnamese give no explanation as to why they are returning the lieutenant's body after fourteen years of denying any knowledge of him.[1]

The story of Lieutenant Dodge is similar to that of Air Force Col. David L. Hrdlicka. You'll recall from chapter 1 that the colonel was shot down over Laos in 1965, after which his photograph was published in the Russian newspaper *Pravda* and a copy of a letter he had written as a prisoner was broadcast over Laotian radio. There is only one difference in the two stories. Colonel Hrdlicka remains among the missing at the time this book was being written.[2]

United States Air Force Col. David L. Hrdlicka, missing in action since 1965. Below: *members of Hrdlicka's family (below) still hope for his return many years later.*

And there is still more evidence of North Vietnamese lies. The late Ohio congressman Tennyson Guyer* was always quick to point out that the North Vietnamese, despite their stubborn insistence of having no knowledge of prisoners, had used the names, pictures, and voices of no fewer than 138 American captives for propaganda purposes.[4]

CLUE #2:
"INDIRECT EVIDENCE"

Many people point to what can be called "indirect evidence" to substantiate their belief that American prisoners are to be found in Southeast Asia. By indirect evidence we mean that there is reason to believe the North Vietnamese are holding U.S. men captive because they have kept the military personnel of other nations imprisoned for long periods of time.

The chief example of such indirect evidence concerns France. A recent British television documentary reported that after the North Vietnamese drove France out of Indochina in 1954, they kept more than 1,000 foreign legionnaires as captives and freed them a few at a time over a span of sixteen years. During that time, so the documentary contended, France annually paid a ransom of several million dollars for their release.

The French government, however, has branded the British report as untrue and has said that the men were not prisoners but soldiers who had elected to remain in Southeast Asia because they liked the area or had started families there. Additionally, the government has insisted that it never paid any money for their release.[5] But are the French to be believed, or are they trying to "save face" by denying that they handed over millions of dollars in ransom? Only those French officials who are "in the know" about the situation can say.

---

*Representative Guyer died in 1981. He was one of the five House Select Committee members who objected to the final committee report in 1976 and urged President Carter to continue seeking the return of living POWs.[3]

Another example of indirect evidence and also of a Vietnamese lie:

After their departure from Indochina, the French are particularly interested in learning the fate of one missing soldier. The North Vietnamese claim no knowledge of him but have to change their story when the French not only learn that the young man is dead but also pinpoint the exact cemetery in which he is buried. The North Vietnamese then admit knowing of the young soldier but say that his body cannot be recovered because of bad weather and the difficult terrain in which the cemetery is located. Why are the French so interested in the young soldier? He is the grandson of Gen. Charles De Gaulle, the leader of the Free French movement in World War II and twice the president of France (1945–46 and 1958–69).[6]

Still more evidence, again from the French experience with the North Vietnamese:

In 1968, a soldier escapes from a Vietcong prison in South Vietnam. He claims to have been held captive since 1954, a period of fourteen years.[7]

And still more, this time from another source:

When Saigon falls to the North Vietnamese in 1975, they are accused of taking a South Korean diplomat, Rhee Dai Yong, prisoner. The North Vietnamese deny the charge for years, even when the Korean government produces a photograph of Rhee in captivity. Their denials continue until 1980 when, after negotiations with Korea, they finally release the diplomat. On being freed, Rhee says that he had once been told that two young Americans were being held in the same prison as he. He calls them victims of Vietnamese "hostage diplomacy," his term for what many an American is calling "economic blackmail," the bartering of U.S. aid for their release.[8]

That the North Vietnamese have held the personnel of other nations, especially France, for such long periods has brought a telling comment on the American MIA/POW issue from Sen. John McCain of Arizona. As you'll recall from chapter 3, Mr. McCain was himself a Vietnam prisoner for five years. He recently remarked that, in light of the French experience, there will always be the suspicion that living Americans are being held somewhere in Southeast Asia. The worry over our missing men, he said, will not end until there is as full an accounting as is possible of all lost Americans.[9]

CLUE #3:
MYSTERIOUS HAPPENINGS

The suspicion that Americans are still being held prisoner in Southeast Asia is further heightened by a number of mysterious happenings that have occurred though the years. Here are two examples.

The Mystery of
the Returned Package

In June 1969, navy pilot Capt. Michael J. Estocin crashed near the city of Haiphong in North Vietnam.[10] Enemy radio broadcasts that were picked up by American monitors the next day indicated that the captain had been captured soon after the crash. His family, on hearing that he had been taken prisoner, began sending him packages of food, toiletries, and

Sen. John McCain holds a photograph of a monument that the Vietnamese erected in Hanoi in regard to his capture there during the war. In 1985 he returned to Vietnam to take part in a special telecast for the tenth anniversary of the fall of Saigon.

other items that he might need to make his life in captivity more bearable. All the packages were addressed to the captain in care of the government of the Democratic Republic of North Vietnam. All were returned unopened.

Then 1972 brought a mystery. One returned package had a small hole punched in it. On opening the package, the Estocin family found a small handmade baby bootee inside. Fastened to the bootee were two felt letters—two *M*s—and three red hearts. The family felt certain that the captain had sent them a message. They said that the *M*s could stand for the first-name initials of the captain and his wife—Mike and Marie. The three hearts, they believed, stood for the couple's three children.

Though the package and its mysterious contents were received more than fifteen years ago, the Estocin family continues to think, and hope, that the captain is still alive.

The "52" Mystery

In 1981, while studying a series of satellite photographs taken above Laos, U.S. government analysts raised their eyebrows in surprise. The photos revealed a stockade with wooden towers along its borders in a jungle area and indicated that it might be housing American prisoners.[11]

The indications were several. They began with the fact that the photographs showed people sitting and moving about the site. A number of the figures cast shadows that revealed them to be taller than the average Laotian. Some were handling tools thought too large for use by the Laotians. And some were sitting cross-legged on the ground rather than squatting down on their haunches as is customary with the Laotians.

Most startling of all, however, was that a number of the pictures showed the figure 52 outlined on the ground. Built of logs, the figure caused much discussion among the analysts. Did it mean that members of a downed B-52 bomber were being held in the camp? Or did it mean that the camp housed fifty-two prisoners?

Captain Michael Estocin, who has been missing in action since 1969.

Michael's sister-in-law Shirley holds the baby bootee and red hearts she believes Michael sent.

Whatever the answer might be, the CIA decided that the stockade must be investigated. The CIA organized a band of twenty to thirty Laotian mercenary soldiers in Thailand, trained them, and then dispatched them over the border to hunt for the site. In the end, the group made two forays into Laos.

On their first attempt, they were driven back out by Laotian gunfire. They returned a month later. This time, two of their number made their way to the compound. After searching the place and taking photographs of the inmates there, they returned with disheartening news. They had found no American prisoners. And they had found no evidence of Americans ever having been there. On the basis of what the two had and had not seen, the United States concluded that the installation was most likely a "reeducation camp" for Laotian political prisoners.

But, to this day, many people doubt this conclusion. They wonder if the Laotian government, on hearing of the planned forays, moved the U.S. prisoners to another location and then cleared the stockade of all signs that Americans had ever been there. And what of that 52 outlined in logs? What it meant and why it was constructed there in the Laotian jungle have remained unsolved mysteries through the years.

A LAST QUESTION

It's time now to turn from the living MIAs to the dead. But before we do so, a final question needs to be asked.

The North Vietnamese, as you know, began to withhold information on the MIAs and POWs in 1973 when President Nixon changed his position on his proffered $3.25 billion in aid. The United States charged that they were using the missing men as pawns in a game of "economic blackmail." In the end, the $3.25 billion was never paid.

That the United States was not going to pay the money became very clear to the North Vietnamese in a matter of months. They saw the question of the aid put aside and then forgotten as America's leadership and its population became deeply involved in the Watergate scandal that ended with Mr. Nixon's resignation from the presidency. The reason for holding the missing men evaporated; yet the North Vietnamese continued to do so. If the suspicions are correct, they have gone on doing so for years with living prisoners. And, as we'll see in the next chapter, they have certainly gone on doing so with the remains of dead MIAs.

And so the question must be asked: Why, when the reason for this course of action evaporated so long ago, have the North Vietnamese insisted on holding all these men, both living and dead?

Several possible answers have been suggested over the years. For one, some people think that even at this late date the former enemy still clings to the hope of one day exchanging the living and the dead for American aid. For another, there is the belief that the North Vietnamese are simply a cruel people who, despite once having said they wanted to return the missing for "humanitarian" reasons, care little for human life and think nothing of keeping prisoners for years.

It is also likely, many people argue, that the North Vietnamese are afraid to return the missing Americans, especially those who may yet be alive. After years of contending that they hold no captives, they know they would be viewed as liars by the world should they now permit a return. They would "lose face"—in the Asian mind, the worst of all humiliations. Moreover, they would have to endure hearing the prisoners tell the world of the hardships they suffered at the hands of the North Vietnamese.

Finally, there is the belief that the Americans are being held because they can provide certain technical skills that the enemy lacks and because they are needed for the maintenance of some equipment with which the Vietnamese are unfamiliar. This belief, which is based in part on reports received from Southeast Asia, holds that the American prisoners have long been made to work on construction and engineering projects and on the repair of U.S. automotive, aircraft, and communications equipment captured during the war.[12]

Of these various answers, which may be true? At the moment, no one can say for certain. Perhaps we'll find out one day in the future.

Chapter Six
THE DEAD:
A Tangled Web

America's quest to bring home its dead MIAs is a story in which two parts are entangled as if they were threads. Together, they have created a web of events and suspicions over the years. One part of the story deals with what many Americans see as a deceit shown by the Vietnamese. The other consists of a series of political steps taken by the United States, Vietnam, Laos, and Cambodia in the years since the Vietnam War ended.

VIETNAMESE DECEIT

A sad fact must be faced concerning the MIAs who died in the war and whose bodies were not recovered at its end. The remains of many, if not most, will never be found and returned to the United States. This is because so many men were torn to bits in such tragedies as artillery barrages and air crashes. Their remains, and those of the unfortunates who disappeared in heavy jungle growth, are simply beyond recovery.[1]

But countless Americans believe there are other victims of the war whose remains *can* be returned home but are being deliberately withheld by Vietnam. Much evidence is at hand to support this view. For example, there is the testimony that a South Vietnamese refugee gave some years ago to a U.S. Senate group discussing the MIA problem. He was a mortician, and he claimed to have once seen the bodies of more than 400 Americans. They were stored in a warehouse within the confines of a Hanoi prison. During the war the prison was known to its American inmates as "The Plantation." [2]

Also widespread in the United States is the belief that the Vietnamese have much information on deceased MIAs and are keeping it to themselves. Again, here is a view that is supported by much evidence. For instance, as you'll recall from chapter 2, there is that statement made in 1973 by a North Vietnamese member of the Joint Military Team in charge of the MIA problem. When speaking to an American officer one day, he admitted that his country knew of many dead MIAs. Then he said that since the United States had done so much harm in the war, Vietnam saw no reason to return them just because the United States wanted them.

By themselves, that statement and the report of the refugee mortician stand as sufficient proof to many that the Vietnamese have been deceitful in their handling of the MIA/POW issue. Both indicate that dead MIAs will not be returned until the Vietnamese are paid the $3.25 billion in aid proffered by President Nixon in 1973 or until some other sort of aid is received. To legions of concerned Americans, the situation appears to be what it has always been suspected of being: a case of "economic blackmail."

In fact, the Vietnamese have returned a number of remains to American hands through the years. But the returns have done little to ease the suspicion of deceit. This is because many of the remains were of men about whom the United States had earlier asked the Vietnamese. The Vietnamese had met all the inquiries with the stubborn insistence that they knew nothing of the men. Then, sometimes years later, they had surrendered the remains—customarily without a word of explanation.

It is possible that the Vietnamese did not know about these men at the time of the inquiries and then came upon them later. However, the silence that accompanied the returns certainly indicates otherwise.

Remember the case of the navy's Lt. Ron Dodge in chapter 5? His plane was shot down while over Vietnam on April 18, 1967. That very day, a North Vietnamese radio broadcast reported the flier's capture. Later, he was used in a propaganda film. Yet, for years, the North Vietnamese denied any knowledge of Lieutenant Dodge, after which they returned his body without explanation in 1981—exactly fourteen years and fifty-one days after his plane went down. It makes no sense whatsoever to do anything but greet their denials with scorn.

Those Who Have Been Returned

In the years since 1973 the Vietnamese have returned the remains of some 200 American servicemen.[3] Often, the remains have belonged to men lost in flaming air crashes and have been nothing more than bits of bone and teeth.

As of early 1988, the army's Central Identification Laboratory (CIL) claimed to have identified 173 MIAs from those 200 sets of remains.[4]* Some of the other sets are still under study, and still others have been designated as unidentifiable.

As its name indicates, the CIL is charged with examining all returned remains and determining that they belong to spe-

---

*The 173 identifications are not only of MIAs whose remains have been returned by the Vietnamese but also of men whose remains have been located by U.S. teams while searching several air-crash sites in both Vietnam and Laos. Those searches will be described in chapter 7.

There is a reason for saying that the CIL *claims* to have made all these identifications rather than simply stating that the laboratory *made* them. As we'll soon see, the laboratory's work methods have long been under fire. Until late 1986 many of its identifications were in question.

cific men. The laboratory is housed in a small barrackslike building near Hawaii's Pearl Harbor and is manned by military and civilian technicians.

Here is a year-by-year listing of the 173 identifications claimed by the CIL through the years:[5]

1974:	23	1979:	0	1984:	6
1975:	5	1980:	1	1985:	50
1976:	2	1981:	3	1986:	21
1977:	33	1982:	5	1987:	1
1978:	12	1983:	9	1988:	2 (as of Feb.)

Five sets of remains were returned in 1987—three in September and two in November. The September returns netted the identifications of three air force officers. The November returns are still under study. The three air force officers identified were Maj. Roger E. Behnfelt, Lt. Col. Wayne Fullam, and Maj. Michael J. Bosiljevac. The word of Major Behnfelt's identification was released in December 1987. Lieutenant Colonel Fullam's identification was announced in January 1988; Major Bosiljevac's, on February 5, 1988.[6]

POLITICS AND THE DEAD

The CIL cannot attempt identifications unless it is given remains to identify. The identifications claimed in a given year always indicate the number of remains most recently received. It is interesting to note how the number of identifications—and, hence, the number of remains being returned—has corresponded to changes in America's political relations with Vietnam, Laos, and Cambodia.

The number has fluctuated on the basis of whether those relations have been looking good or bad. Though the United States and the Socialist Republic of Vietnam have never been on good terms since the war's end, the number of returned remains has gone up and the identifications have increased when the relations have seemed to be improving. The returns and the identifications have fallen when the relations have worsened.

To see what is meant here, we need to divide the years and their identifications as follows:[7]

1974:	23	1976:	2	1979:	0
1975:	5	1977:	33	1980:	1
	28	1978:	12		1
			47		

1981:	3
1982:	5
1983:	9
1984:	6
1985:	50
1986:	21
1987:	1
1988:	2 (as of Feb.)
	97

To begin, consider the twenty-eight sets of remains that were identified in 1974 and 1975. Twenty-three of their number were received by the Americans when the members of the Joint Military Team were working together to resolve the MIA/ POW issue. But then came the violations of the cease-fire pact and the problem of President Nixon's "broken promise" to provide the former enemy with $3.25 billion in aid. Vietnamese cooperation evaporated; the number of remains being returned quickly fell off, with only five identifications reported in 1975.

As was discussed in chapter 2, the late 1970s saw President Carter seek to improve Washington's relations with Vietnam in the hopes of bringing stability to a still troubled Southeast Asia. He also wanted to position the United States so that it could take advantage of some economic benefits available from Vietnam, among them the rich oil deposits off its coasts. During that period—the years 1976–1978—the return of MIA remains accelerated, enabling the CIL to claim forty-seven identifications. Then, in 1979, the campaign for better relations disintegrated. A drop in the returns followed immediately. The CIL recorded not a single identification in 1979 and just one in 1980.

By far the greatest number of returns has been recorded since 1981, allowing the CIL to claim ninety-seven identifications between 1981 and early 1988. What accounts for this increase? There are several reasons.

Reagan's "Highest Priority"

First, President Ronald Reagan has shown a great interest in resolving the MIA/POW problem. His interest was voiced in January 1983, when he pledged that his administration would give the search for the MIAs and POWs "the highest national priority."[8] The president repeated his pledge in 1987. In a message to the eighteenth annual meeting of the NLF, he said:

> Tonight, I reaffirm our unwavering commitment to resolving the POW/MIA issue as a matter of highest priority. . . . History will record what we did was right, certain that whoever follows us in office cannot ignore what we have started and accomplished.[9]

Exactly what Mr. Reagan's administration has accomplished in his commitment to resolve the MIA/POW issue will be the subject of chapter 8.

For the time being, all we need to know is that his interest has helped to net an increase in the number of American remains being returned by the Vietnamese.

But Mr. Reagan's interest, while it has helped, cannot be given all the credit for the increasing return of MIA remains. Another reason is also in play; it has to do with the economic picture in Vietnam.

A former prisoner of war, Ralph Gaither (left), presents President Reagan with a plaque from the National League of Families after the President promised the group he would give the search for MIAs and POWs the "highest national priority."

Vietnam and Its Economy

The Vietnamese economy has been in difficulty for years. The country has been receiving foreign aid annually since the end of the war. That aid, however, has not been of the type that would help the country to grow economically. Consequently, Vietnam has been forced to go deeply into debt to support itself.[10]

During the war, the northerners were helped financially by China and a few Western nations, among them Sweden and Denmark. Since then, however, the bulk of the country's aid has come from the Soviet Union. Most of the aid has been in the form of military equipment and supplies. The Soviets have not provided the Vietnamese with the consumer goods and the technological assistance needed to develop a strong economy. The result of all this is that Vietnam needs U.S. assistance. Its return of an increasing number of MIA remains in the 1980s is seen by many Americans as a strategy for eventually gaining the needed U.S. aid.

Such aid, however, can come only with what is called a "normalization" of relations between the United States and Vietnam—meaning the establishment of diplomatic ties between the two nations and the opening of embassies and consular offices within each other's boundaries. There have never been such ties. If established, they could not only open the door to U.S. aid but could also pave the way to future assistance from countries friendly to the United States—among them, Japan and several European countries. Again, Vietnam's cooperation in the MIA/POW quest is seen as a strategy, this one meant to hasten normalization.

When President Carter attempted to better America's relations with Vietnam in the 1970s, he, too, was trying to "normalize" ties between the two countries. The Reagan administration is as interested in normalization as was Mr. Carter, and for much the same reasons. But there is a major difference between the two men as far as the POW/MIA issue is concerned.

Mr. Carter saw the resolution of the MIA/POW issue as a part of the normalization process. This meant that if anything stalled the process, the MIA/POW issue would likewise be stalled. But when Mr. Reagan said the POW/MIA issue was to be given the "highest priority," he made it a humanitarian issue that is quite apart and separate from the normalization process.[11] If anything now goes amiss with the efforts toward normalization, the quest for the return of the living and dead MIAs will still be pursued. This fact, it is widely believed, has not been lost on the Vietnamese and has helped to prompt them to an increasing cooperation in the MIA/POW issue.

Vietnam and the Cambodian Problem

A third reason for the increased cooperation brings us to a situation that is both political and economic. Though supplied by the Chinese during the war, the Vietnamese have traditionally looked on China as a great enemy and today it still sees its giant neighbor as its greatest enemy. Much of the present enmity stems from events in recent years in Cambodia.[12]

In 1975, the political faction known as the Khmer Rouge took control of Cambodia, establishing a harsh regime that caused thousands of people to flee the nation. The Khmer Rouge leaders turned to China as an ally and then rebelled against the influence that North Vietnam had long exerted in their country. Their rebellion saw them engage in a number of skirmishes over the lands along the Cambodian-Vietnamese border.

The Vietnamese, however, were determined to regain the upper hand in Cambodia. And so they sent their troops pouring into the country in late 1978. During the opening days of 1979, the capital city of Phnom Penh fell before the onslaught. Placed in power was a group of men who had broken with the Khmer Rouge and were sympathetic to Vietnam.

The new government renamed the nation the People's Republic of Kampuchea.*

Ever since the takeover, the forces of the deposed Khmer Rouge, with the help of supporters within the country and with Chinese aid, have fought to overthrow the Vietnamese-backed government. At the same time, the United States and China have improved their relations, a fact that alarms Vietnam. The Vietnamese, by bettering their own relations with the United States, hope to alleviate the dangers that a close American alliance with such an enemy as China poses for them. An increasing cooperation in the return of MIA remains could help to better those relations.

Finally, in the eyes of many nations, the presence of Vietnamese troops in Cambodia has made Vietnam appear to be an aggressor nation.[13] The Reagan administration has said that a normalization of relations with Vietnam cannot come until there is a political settlement in Cambodia. By "political settlement," Mr. Reagan means that Vietnam must withdraw its troops from Cambodia.[14] For several years, the Vietnamese were thought to be using their increased cooperation in the MIA/POW quest as a way of softening the U.S. demand here and moving toward a normalization of relations without removing their troops from Cambodia. As one Washington official put it, the MIA/POW issue was the only significant leverage that the Vietnamese could apply to get the United States to do what they want.[15]

Cambodia has long been called "Vietnam's Vietnam." In the years following the 1979 invasion, Vietnam lost some 25,000 men in the Cambodian fighting. The fighting proved such a burden and the need for normal relations with the United

---

*In the years immediately prior to the installation of the new government, Cambodia underwent another name change and was known as Democratic Kampuchea. Throughout this book, we have referred to the country as Cambodia and will continue to do so. This is because many nations have refused to recognize its newest name and because, of the two names, Cambodia is the more familiar.

States grew so great that, in 1988, Vietnam announced it would withdraw its forces. Hanoi said that it planned to pull 50,000 troops out in 1988 and would complete the withdrawal of all its troops by 1990.[16]

Laos

Vietnam is not the only country in Southeast Asia facing economic difficulties. Also in financial trouble is Laos. Much of its problem stems from the fact that it suffered a disastrously poor rice crop in 1984. Laos has recently joined Vietnam in giving more cooperation than ever before to the quest for America's missing (556 U.S. servicemen who disappeared in Laos during the war). The Laotian government is thought to be doing so in the hope of receiving economic help from a grateful Washington.

In fact, Washington has already supplied Laos with a certain amount of aid. In the wake of 1984's poor rice crop, the United States dispatched 5,000 tons of rice to Laos.[17]

A BANNER YEAR

The year 1985 stands as a banner year in the new cooperation shown by Vietnam. It was marked by sudden and surprising news from Hanoi: the announcement that the Vietnamese planned, in their words, "to accelerate" the work on resolving the MIA issue and hoped to have the whole matter settled once and for all in just two years. In Washington, the announcement was widely viewed as a response to the "highest priority" that President Reagan had given the MIA quest and as an indication of how desperately Vietnam needed U.S. financial aid.

The announcement, which was made in the first half of the year, was followed by another surprise. On July 4, a Vietnamese Foreign Ministry official, Cuu Dinh Ba, met with a U.S. delegation that had come to Hanoi to discuss the "accelerated" efforts on behalf of the MIAs. Ba brought out a list containing the names of twenty-six missing Americans.

Saying that their bodies had been found recently in the nation's provinces, Ba promised to return them to U.S. authorities in perhaps six to eight weeks. Additionally, Ba said that Vietnam would provide the United States with information and "evidence" regarding the fates of six other MIAs.[18]

Action followed his words within a month. In August 1985, a U.S. military delegation accepted the flag-draped caskets containing the remains of the twenty-six men. The bodies were the most ever turned over to American hands at one time since the end of the war.[19]

But Vietnamese action did not end with the return of the twenty-six MIAs. Before 1985 drew to a close, Vietnam gave permission for a U.S. search team to visit the site of an air crash and locate the remains of the men who had died there. It was the first such permission granted in the twelve years since the death of Capt. Richard M. Rees at a crash site in December 1973. Through the years, the Americans had asked for permission to conduct searches. All the requests had been denied or ignored.

Vietnam was not alone in 1985 when it granted permission for a search. Laos also permitted a U.S. investigation of an air-crash site that year and then gave its approval for a 1986 investigation. These searches will be discussed in the next chapter.

Chapter Seven
THE DEAD: Discoveries and Doubts

The U.S. searches of air-crash sites in Vietnam and Laos yielded thousands of bone fragments. The overwhelming majority were unearthed at the Laos sites, with the Vietnam site yielding some eighteen fragments which proved to be unidentifiable. The two Laos investigations resulted in the CIL claiming to make more than twenty positive identifications of dead MIAs.[1] The identifications, however, were met with widespread public doubt, and the CIL's work came under harsh attack.

In this chapter we are going to look first at the investigations and what they discovered and then at the reasons why so many people have doubted the CIL's Laos identifications. By a margin of just a few months, Laos beat Vietnam to the punch in granting permission in 1985 for a crash-site investigation.

LAOS: THE PAKSE SITE

As you'll recall from chapter 1, enemy ground fire punctured a fuel line in a U.S. Air Force AC-130 gunship while the plane was flying above North Vietnam on a December night in 1972. As the gunship was limping back to its base in Thailand, it exploded and crashed in a dense jungle area about 25 miles (40 km) northeast of the Laotian city of Pakse. Two crewmen parachuted to safety and were rescued. Their fourteen fellow airmen went down with the flaming aircraft. A rescue helicopter made its way to the crash site the following day and found the partial remains—a forearm and hand—of one man. Because there was no trace of the thirteen remaining men, they were thought to have been incinerated in the crash and were officially listed as MIAs.

Some years later, in the early 1980s, Washington began to negotiate with the Laotian government for permission to visit the downed plane and search for the remains of its thirteen missing crewmen. The negotiations bore some fruit in 1982 when the Laotians, as a goodwill gesture, permitted a visit to the site by a delegation from the NLF. An actual investigation of the twisted and burned plane was not allowed at that time.

However, in July 1984, after further negotiations, the Laotian government agreed to an actual investigation at some date in the future. Permission to make the investigation was finally granted in early February 1985.[2]*

It is interesting to note that final permission was awarded just a few months after the United States had donated 5,000 tons of rice to help Laos recover from its poor 1984 harvest. A number of U.S. officials believed that the permission added up to a "thank you" for the rice. They also suspected that

*The negotiations were facilitated by the fact that, unlike its relations with the Socialist Republic of Vietnam, the United States has maintained some diplomatic ties with Laos. They have been what are called "low level" ties, meaning that they have not involved U.S. diplomats of the highest rank.[3]

the Laotians might be trying to open the door to better relations with the United States and the possibility of further American aid. In commenting on this latter belief, one Washington official said that more than a single permission for a site examination would be needed before the United States would commit itself to additional aid. For that, he remarked, the Laotians would have to come up with a sustained pattern of cooperation.[4]

Within days of receiving the permission, the United States sent a twelve-man search team to the Pakse site.[5] Accompanied by Laotian soldiers, they worked for two weeks at the scene, pulling aside pieces of wreckage and digging into the surrounding earth to find what they could of the men who had perished there more than a dozen years earlier. All that they unearthed were bits of bone and teeth plus a smattering of battered and charred personal effects that had once belonged to the crewmen.

During a visit to the site, *Time* correspondent James Willwerth described many of the bone fragments as looking like pieces of gray pumice (volcanic glass filled with holes and light in weight) because they had been incinerated in the crash. Some of the fragments were no more than the size of a cigar stub. Willwerth said that to the untrained eye the fragments would be difficult to identify as bones.

The bone and teeth fragments found at the site have been variously reported as numbering from 50,000 to 65,000. Whatever their exact total, they were flown to the CIL in Hawaii. The civilian and military workers there separated them into piles and identified each pile as belonging to a specific man. The CIL announced it had positively identified the thirteen Pakse victims.

LAOS: THE SAVANNAKHET SITE

The investigation of what is called the Savannakhet site involved another U.S. AC-130 gunship.[6] The plane was struck by an enemy ground-to-air missile in 1972 while on a reconnaissance (exploratory military survey of enemy territory) mission near the border separating Laos from North Vietnam. It crashed in the Laotian jungle about 80 miles (128 km) east of the city of Savannakhet. Savannakhet itself lies some 100 miles (160 km) north of Pakse. Fourteen men went down with the ship.

The Laotian government permitted a U.S. search team to investigate the site in February 1986—fourteen years after the plane crashed and exactly one year after the Pakse search. The team, which included four men from the CIL, was assisted by fifteen Laotian soldiers. The searchers began their work by clearing the area of still potentially dangerous machine-gun ammunition and cannon shells. Next, they divided the site into 20-foot (2-m) squares and marked off each square with tape. Then they painstakingly investigated each square. First, they looked for the most visible objects—large bone fragments and personal gear such as pocket knives, sidearms, and dog tags. Then they dug in the earth for smaller fragments of bone and teeth. Among the larger items found was a dog tag imprinted with the name of Capt. Richard Castillo, who was serving as the operator of the doomed plane's infrared sensor.

The search lasted for ten days and yielded about 5,000 fragments. Some were as small as rice kernels, while the largest measured about 3 inches (8 cm) long. The fragments went to the CIL for study. They yielded identifications of eight of the fourteen men. The remaining victims have yet to be identified.

VIETNAM: THE YEN THUONG SITE

In chapter 1 an incident was described in which, during a December night in 1972, a U.S. Air Force B-52 was struck by an antiaircraft missile and crashed into the tiny village of Yen Thuong, some 9 miles (15 km) northwest of Hanoi. As the ship fell, two crewmen parachuted into the jungle, where they were captured by enemy troops, later to be released in the prisoner exchange that followed the signing of the cease-fire pact. Four other crewmen failed to escape and, though thought assuredly dead, were listed as MIA.[7]

Nearly thirteen years later, the Vietnamese government, as part of its "accelerated" program to resolve the MIA issue, allowed an American team of eleven men to investigate the crash site. The investigation was conducted in December 1985 and saw the team members dig out the earth at the center of the wreckage an inch (3 cm) at a time with knives. Located with the help of North Vietnamese assistants was a collection of about eighteen bone fragments. As mentioned earlier, they proved too small to be identifiable when sent to the CIL.

IDENTIFICATIONS
AND DOUBTS

Throughout the years since 1973, whenever Vietnam has returned the shattered remains of missing men and the CIL has identified them, many of their families have accepted the identifications without question. On receiving the remains, they have quietly buried them and have begun to rebuild their lives after what had seemed to be an eternity of anguish and uncertainty. Others have doubted the identifications and have gone on pressing the government for information on their lost ones.

Much the same can be said of the families of the Pakse crash victims who had been positively identified. Some took the CIL at its word, but several did not. They decided to check on the identifications to see if they had any merit to them.

What they found shocked the nation. They came up with evidence that the identifications had been poorly made and were, as a consequence, very likely incorrect. Since the CIL was run by the military, this finding prompted countless

Americans to suspect the government of still trying to "close the books" on the MIA issue as quickly as possible. To them, President Reagan's promise to give the problem the "highest priority" suddenly had a hollow ring to it.

In the eyes of many, the CIL was making groundless identifications for the military just to get the MIAs buried and forgotten. Others did not agree with this view but held that the CIL must be an inept facility. Whatever the truth, the laboratory came under fire from two directions—first, from several MIA families and then from Washington itself.

The Hart Case

We begin with the case of Mrs. Anne Hart of Florida.[8] Her husband, Lt. Col. Thomas Hart III, was aboard the AC-130 gunship when it went down at Pakse. The CIL, after separating the thousands of bone and teeth fragments found at the site, announced that it had positively identified those of Colonel Hart. Mrs. Hart greeted the finding with doubt. For years, she had suspected that her husband had survived the crash.

She felt her suspicion was wellfounded. To begin with, a few years after the crash, the army informed her that a military unit friendly to the United States had found five opened parachutes near the Pakse site. This indicated that the two men who had parachuted from the doomed ship had been joined by others. There was a good chance that one of their number had been her husband.

Raising her hopes even more was another piece of news. In July 1973 a reconnaissance plane had photographed an area about 100 miles (160 km) from the Pakse site. The photographs revealed a strange message burned in the ground. The message consisted of 20-foot (6-m)-long letters and numbers. They read either *1973 TH* or *1953 TH*. The numbers could have indicated the year or could have been some sort of military identification number. Far more important to Mrs. Hart were the letters *TH;* they were the same as her husband's initials.

The army made an analysis of the message and said that

it could not have been etched in the ground by Colonel Hart. Mrs. Hart then learned that the army had destroyed the original report of the message. From that time on, all her inquiries about the message were met with silence. She strongly suspected the army, in its desire to "close the books" on the MIA issue, of withholding information on her husband from her.

And so, on hearing that the CIL had positively identified the colonel's remains, Mrs. Hart turned to a noted forensic scientist, Dr. Michael Charney, for help. (Forensic scientists study the remains or the bodies of the deceased for such purposes as identification and the cause of death.) She asked Dr. Charney to examine her husband's supposed remains, which had been flown from the CIL's headquarters in Hawaii to the military mortuary at Oakland, California.

Dr. Charney, who is the director of the Center of Human Identification at Colorado State University, agreed to Mrs. Hart's request. He said later that he had no reason to doubt the competence of the CIL at the start of his examination. But what he then saw shocked him—and his report of his findings shocked Mrs. Hart and the relatives of the other men missing at Pakse.

Colonel Hart's remains had consisted of a mere seven bone fragments which ranged in length from less than 1 inch (3 cm) to about 6 inches (18 cm). In just these few bones, the CIL claimed to have detected signs of the deceased's age, sex, and race. It had determined that they came from a male Caucasian who was between thirty and thirty-five years of age, stood 5 feet, 9 inches (175 cm) tall, and had a slightly larger than average build. On comparing its findings with the known characteristics of the men aboard the AC-130 gunship, the CIL claimed that the bone fragments definitely came from Colonel Hart's body.

Dr. Charney reported that there was no way a positive identification could have been made from the few fragments. They were simply too small for an identification. The doctor called the laboratory's work the worst sort of incompetence.

The Fuller Case

The criticism of the CIL did not end with Dr. Charney's report. The laboratory then ran into trouble with Donald Parker of Oregon. He was the nephew of Sgt. James R. Fuller, who had served aboard the AC-130 as flight engineer and whose bone fragments had been positively identified.[9]

When a coffin bearing Sergeant Fuller's remains was returned to the United States, Parker took possession of it and flew it to the family home for burial. But, as suspicious of the CIL findings as was Mrs. Hart, Parker had the coffin opened prior to burial. Within, he found a cotton sheet. Beneath it lay a new army tunic. On the tunic were twenty-eight bone fragments.

Parker was stunned by what he saw. He said that the fragments could be held in the palm of one hand and that the largest of their number were about thumb-size. There was nothing about the bones, Parker added, that could enable someone to say that they looked as if they belonged to a human being. He turned immediately to Dr. Charney.

For a second time, Dr. Charney issued a disturbing report. He said that the bone fragments were mostly human in origin but that several were questionable and that one was *not* of human origin. Nothing, he concluded, could be determined with certainty as to the deceased person's sex, race, physical build, and time of death.

The Fanning Case

More trouble now cropped up for the CIL. This time, it had nothing to do with the Pakse identifications. Rather, it concerned marine flier Hugh Fanning, who was listed as MIA after his plane was shot down over Vietnam in 1967.[10]

When the Vietnamese returned the remains of a number of MIAs in 1984, the CIL positively identified those of the marine flier as being among them. When his wife, Mrs. Kathryn Fanning of Oklahoma, learned something about them, she was immediately suspicious of the identification—and for a strange reason.

During the years the flier was listed as missing, Mrs. Fanning had often dreamed of her husband. In one of those dreams, he told her that he suffered a hole in his head. Mrs. Fanning had such a deep faith in her dreams that she asked an officer associated with the return of her husband's remains if they included a skull with a hole made by a bullet or a piece of shrapnel. The officer answered that the skull showed no signs of such a wound.

This news was upsetting, but a greater upset followed. Mrs. Fanning found that she had been told a lie. She learned that a skull was not listed among her husband's remains, a fact that would have been known to the officer to whom she had talked. In all, the remains consisted of just thirty bone fragments. Together they added up to a mere 15 percent of the bones in an average adult skeleton. Was this another case of the government trying, with the help of its military, to "close the books" on the MIA issue by declaring a missing man as identified so that he could be buried and forgotten?

Knowing that she had no idea whether the fragments actually came from her husband, Mrs. Fanning did as Anne Hart and Donald Parker had done. She sought out a forensic scientist and asked him to examine the fragments.

The scientist to whom she turned was Dr. Clyde Snow. His examination ended in a report that was as troubling as those of Dr. Charney. Dr. Snow said that the bones belonged to a young white male. But, he explained, they were so few as to make a positive identification impossible.

THE CIL UNDER INVESTIGATION

U.S. military officials disagreed with the Charney and Snow reports. They insisted that the CIL's identifications of marine pilot Fanning and the Pakse victims had been sound. In the Fanning case, they said, the CIL's identification had been supported by information from the Vietnamese. On being questioned about the flier's remains, the Hanoi government had assured the United States that they had been found along with those of his copilot at the spot where the two crashed.[11]

However, the storm of criticism over the identifications—plus the fact that the growing Vietnamese and Laotian cooperation promised to bring an increasing number of returns in the future—caused the military to take a closer look at its CIL.[12] It employed a team of civilian scientists to study the laboratory. The team members were to determine if it could handle a heavier caseload and were to submit recommendations for any necessary improvements. They visited the lab between December 9 and 12, 1985, found its staff to be well trained, but said that, in great part, its facilities and equipment ranged from inadequate to barely adequate. Their recommendation: Employ additional staff and install better equipment.

Though finding the staff well trained, the team members did not like the methods of identification employed by the lab's chief, Tadao Furue. Furue, a Japanese scientist, had been working for the U.S. government since 1951 and had won much public attention in 1983 when he identified the remains of twenty-two men who died in the Pacific island crash of an air force plane during World War II. His staff's positive identifications of those men, and then of the Pakse victims and the MIAs who had been returned through the years by the Vietnamese, had all been based on a work method that he called "morphological approximation." Furue claimed that the procedures used in "morphological approximation" enabled him to achieve definite identifications from just a few bone chips.

A Useless Method

The team members condemned Furue's method as useless. They pointed out that forensic scientists are able to take just a few *complete* bones and, based on a knowledge of such characteristics as age and race, make a rough determination of what a person looked like. However, with just those few complete bones, it is usually impossible to come up with such specifics as the victim's height, weight, and sex. When talking of a deceased person's size, for example, forensic scientists will do no more than estimate his height to have been within a certain range—say, from 5 feet 4 inches (162 cm) to 5 feet 8 inches (172 cm).

But Tadao Furue had made positive identifications not with a few *complete* bones but with a smattering of mere bone chips. If forensic scientists had usually found it impossible to be specific with complete bones, then it was more than impossible to be specific with bone chips. There was, the team members said, no known scientific method for making the kinds of identification that Furue was claiming.

As a result of their study, the team members recommended that an internationally respected scientist be employed to head the laboratory. The new chief would supervise the work of Furue and the staff. This recommendation was considered to be the most important of the team's suggestions.

In the next months, the army acted on the various recommendations. Additional workers were hired, and the quality of the laboratory's equipment was upgraded. Furue was told to drop his use of "morphological approximation" and turn to the traditional and time-honored methods of identification.

The military, however, chose not to employ a new chief for the laboratory. Rather, Dr. Ellis R. Keily of the University of Maryland was appointed as a permanent consultant to the lab. Dr. Keily had served as a member of the investigating team. As consultant to the lab, he would review and approve all CIL identifications.

Though the suspicion that the government is still out to "close the books" on the MIA issue continues to persist in many quarters, the investigation of the CIL and the changes that have since gone into effect there have relieved many Americans. In those changes, they see a lessening of mistaken identifications and a reason to think that the government or the military is no longer trying to shunt the MIAs aside but is giving President Reagan's "highest priority" to them.

That the changes have been to the good can be seen in what happened to the bone and teeth fragments recovered from Savannakhet and Yen Thuong crash sites. Both sites were being investigated at about the same time the CIL itself was under investigation. The fragments from Savannakhet yielded only eight out of fourteen possible identifications, with the CIL then admitting that those from Yen Thuong were too small for identification. On another day, all the sets of fragments from both sites might well have been positively identified in error.

Chapter Eight
THE LIVING AND
THE DEAD: A History

For several chapters now, the situations of the living and the dead MIAs have been discussed separately. But there are events and developments that have concerned them both. To achieve a complete picture here, we must now look at some material new to us and also review certain information from earlier in the book.

THE FIRST YEARS

In review, the quest for living and dead MIAs began when the Four-Party Joint Military Team was formed in 1973. The quarrels over the violations of the Paris cease-fire pact and President Nixon's "broken promise" of $3.25 billion in aid for Vietnam damaged the team's efforts and led to its collapse in 1974. In the interim, the remains of no more than twenty-eight deceased MIAs came into American hands.

In 1975, President Gerald Ford, responding to a widespread public concern over the MIA/POW issue, formed the House Select Committee on Missing Persons in Southeast Asia to investigate the matter. The committee's chairman, Rep. G. V. (Sonny) Montgomery of Mississippi, announced in late 1976 that the committee had found no evidence that any Americans were still alive in Southeast Asia. His announcement was met with doubt across the country and was even disputed by half the committee membership. Five members issued a separate report in which they said they had found evidence to suggest that there were, indeed, missing Americans still alive in Southeast Asia.

Representative Montgomery, in his report, stated that his committee felt that perhaps some 150 dead MIAs were being held in Southeast Asia. The five dissident members held the number of deceased MIAs to be far greater.

By the time the Montgomery report was issued, the nation had elected a new president, Jimmy Carter, and the report was sent to him for consideration. Along with it went the report of the five dissident committeemen. President Carter chose to ignore their findings and accepted the Montgomery report, saying that henceforth the country would concentrate on encouraging the former enemy to return the remains of our deceased MIAs.

The Montgomery report and President Carter's decision added fuel to a nationwide suspicion that Washington was trying to "close the books" quickly on the MIAs as part of a campaign to improve (for a number of political and economic reasons) its relations with Vietnam. The suspicion was to persist for years to come.

THE WOODCOCK COMMISSION

Once he had made his decision, President Carter formed a group that he called the Presidential Commission on America's Missing and Unaccounted for in Southeast Asia.[1] Assigned to the group was the task of visiting North Vietnam and negotiating the return of all dead MIAs. The commission was headed by Leonard Woodcock, the former president of the United Auto Workers Union and later to be the U.S. ambassador to China. The commission was soon being called simply the Woodcock Commission.

Woodcock and his fellow members went to Hanoi in March 1977. The visit ended with his announcement that the group agreed with Montgomery's 1976 report: No living Americans were being held in Southeast Asia. Woodcock added the commission's belief that the Vietnamese government was doing its best to account for the dead MIAs.

The announcement added more fuel to the suspicion that Washington was trying to "close the books" on the MIAs. News reports indicated there were solid reasons for the deepening suspicion. It was learned that the commission had not been allowed to travel outside Hanoi. Nor had its members been permitted to talk with the Vietnamese citizenry. Both prohibitions had kept the commission from gathering information that could have thrown much light on the MIA/POW situation.

Perhaps most damaging of all was that, while en route to Hanoi, the commission had stopped at Hawaii. There the members met with Department of Defense officials. The officials showed them a number of files on MIAs thought to be well-known to the Vietnamese, among them Navy Lt. Ron Dodge (see chapters 5 and 7). The commission took the files to Hanoi and could have used them to pressure the Vietnamese into admitting knowledge of the men and perhaps surrendering them to American hands. But not once during their visit did they produce the files.

In all, the Woodcock Commission was accused of being formed not to benefit the missing but to serve two selfish purposes for Washington. It was to soothe a suspicious American public into believing that the government was making a real effort to repatriate the missing. And, as evidenced

Leonard Woodcock (left), head of President Carter's commission, meets with Nguyen Mihn (right), head of the American Department of the Foreign Ministry, in Hanoi.

by the failure to produce those incriminating files, it was to treat the Vietnamese "gently" in the hope of encouraging better relations between the United States and Vietnam.

An action by the Carter administration topped off all the suspicions about the Woodcock Commission. In 1978, as was discussed earlier, the administration ordered that much MIA/POW information be designated as "classified," meaning that it would now be kept secret from the press and public. Hitherto, it had been listed as "unclassified" and had been available to both. Washington contended that the information must be classified because it contained material that could be of value to the Vietnamese and could jeopardize the repatriation of the missing. With the reclassification coming on the heels of the commission's Hanoi visit, many people thought it was prompted by the public anger caused by the outcome of the visit.

STRANGE ADVENTURES

The passing years have seen a number of searches attempted for both the living and the dead. These searches began with the crash-site visits that were conducted in 1973 by the Joint Military Team. Then there was the 1981 hunt into Laos for the Americans thought to be imprisoned in the stockade with the mysterious 52 outlined in logs within its confines. Finally, in 1985 and 1986, there were the investigations of the Pakse, Savannakhet, and Yen Thuong crash sites.

These are not, however, the only MIA/POW searches on record. Three others were attempted. They had no connection with the U.S. government; rather, they were private hunts led by a retired Green Beret officer. They produced, in the history of the quest for the missing men, one of its strangest episodes.

The feeling that Washington was not doing its best for the missing was running particularly high in the late 1970s and early 1980s. Running quite as high because of all the reported sightings of living MIAs was the eagerness of the

MIA families to learn something—anything—of what had happened to their loved ones. Suspicious of the government's motives, they believed that Washington would be of no assistance in their quest. And so they turned to private sources for help.

They turned to what *Newsweek* magazine once called a growing "industry" in Thailand. Its workers were of two types. First, there were Asians—racketeers and refugees desperate for money—who tried to sell the families information about the missing or attempted to peddle them bits of bone said to have come from a loved one. The information usually turned out to be false, being either an outright lie or based on rumor. The bones often proved to be from animals. [2]

Second, there were American daredevils who, for a fee, were willing to steal over the Thai border and rescue the Americans thought to be imprisoned in Laos. These adventurers bombarded the families with letters and telephone calls in an effort to raise money for the rescue missions. The money-raising campaign appalled the leadership of the NLF, who saw the enterprises as nothing more than rip-offs of the families and many other concerned Americans. [3]

Among the adventurers who wanted to launch rescue attempts was the former Green Beret officer Lt. Col. James "Bo" Gritz. His military background, which included being decorated sixty times during the Vietnam War, was impressive and caused a number of families and film celebrities, Clint Eastwood and William Shatner reportedly among the latter, to finance his ventures. With their money in hand, he attempted four rescue missions. [4]

The first two efforts, called Operation Velvet Hammer and Operation Grand Eagle, were called off while still being planned. But not so Operation Lazarus, the third attempt. In late 1982, jumping off from a secret base in Thailand, Gritz led a troop of three Americans and fifteen Laotians into the jungles of western Laos. His plan called for American prisoners to be located and fetched back to safety in a period of fourteen days. On the third day out, however, he was at-

*Lt. Col. James "Bo" Gritz (left) reviews
a map with Laotian guerrilla leaders during
a search for American prisoners of war.*

tacked by a band of Laotian guerrilla fighters. Two of his own Laotians were killed and one American was captured. Gritz and his remaining men fled Laos.

A month later, he paid a ransom of $17,000 for the release of his captured American comrade. Then, after attempting a fourth trek into Laos, he returned to the United States, leaving behind a Thailand furious at him for jeopardizing its neutral position in Southeast Asia by using it as a base for his secret operations. Upon his arrival home, the U.S. House Subcommittee on Asian Affairs summoned him to give evidence of what he had seen and found in Laos.

Gritz brought word of both the living and dead when he appeared before the subcommittee in 1983. He spoke of reports he had heard of MIA prisoners and then showed photographs that he claimed to have taken of Laotian prison camps. He then said that he had brought home a number of MIA bones. His various claims proved to be groundless. The photographs showed not prison compounds but stretches of open Laotian countryside. The bones were tested and found to be those of animals and two Asians. When pressed by the committee members, Gritz admitted he had no real proof that American MIAs were being held captive in Laos.

In all, the former Green Beret officer, though continuing to insist that MIAs were alive in Southeast Asia, stood discredited in the eyes of the committee and the press. To this day, Gritz remains the subject of various controversies. Some people believe that he was telling the truth and look upon him as a hero. Some feel that he was actually working as an undercover government agent, and that Washington, despite wanting to "close the books" on the MIAs, had sent him out to rescue men it well knew were in Laos. Still others contend that he was neither hero nor secret agent but merely an adventurer who wanted to relive the thrills he had known during the war.

The NLF has always scorned Gritz and all like him. At the time of his missions, the United States was negotiating with Laos for permission to investigate the Pakse crash site. The league feared (and still does) that all such daredevil forays would damage not only the Pakse talks but also all other diplomatic actions to retrieve the missing men.

DIPLOMATIC ACTIONS

Diplomatic actions marked the Reagan administration's work for the MIAs. The actions concerned both the living and dead, because President Reagan, on assigning the highest priority to the quest for the missing, promised that a main order of business would be the recovery of any living Americans who might still be in Southeast Asia.

Negotiations with both Vietnam and Laos took shape following President Reagan's highest-priority pledge. Here, year by year, are the most significant of the negotiations and the results they achieved.[5]

1982
VIETNAM
President Reagan sent a U.S. delegation headed by Deputy Assistant Secretary of Defense Richard Armitage to Hanoi. Won there was an agreement to hold four U.S.-Vietnamese meetings a year on the MIA/POW problem. The sessions, which were called "technical meetings," were to be held between representatives of the U.S. Joint Casualty Resolution Center (JCRC) and the Vietnamese Office for Seeking Missing Persons. The JCRC maintains the records of all missing American personnel. The meetings would study all available MIA/POW information and would pave the way for the return of MIA remains.

LAOS
Laos permitted representatives from the NLF to visit the Pakse crash site. They were also allowed to visit a second site. In Washington, Congress passed a resolution in support of Pres-

ident Reagan's efforts on behalf of the MIAs and POWs. The resolution encouraged the United States and Laos to develop further their cooperation in the matter.

1983
VIETNAM

A U.S.-Vietnamese technical meeting in March was highlighted by the Vietnamese announcement that information they had recently collected on twelve MIAs would soon be handed over to the United States. Subsequent meetings resulted in the return of nine sets of remains to American hands. The summer, however, brought trouble. Hanoi, angered at what it considered to be anti-Vietnamese remarks by several U.S. officials, suspended further meetings. The damage was repaired later in the year through talks in New York City with Vietnamese Foreign Minister Nguyen Co Thach.

LAOS

President Reagan opened the year with the statement that the United States was willing to take steps to improve its relations with Laos. He noted, however, that the United States would regard the progress on the MIA/POW issue as a measure of Laotian interest in bettering those relations. The year was marked by five U.S.-Laotian meetings, held in New York and Laos, to discuss the investigation of the Pakse crash site. A U.S. team was permitted to visit another crash site at year's end.

1984
VIETNAM

A U.S. delegation, again headed by Assistant Secretary of Defense Armitage, visited Hanoi in February. Reached during the meetings there was Foreign Minister Thach's agreement to speed the work on the MIA/POW problem. Both sides resolved that the issue should not be jeopardized by any American-Vietnamese quarrels and differences. As a result of the talks, the JCRC and the Vietnamese Office for Seeking

Missing Persons resumed their technical meetings. The mid-year saw eight sets of remains turned over to the United States. Of that number, six were identified as those of MIAs.

LAOS
Laos agreed to the investigation of the Pakse crash site. Two congressional delegations visited Laos and, among other topics discussed, raised the MIA/POW issue.

1985
VIETNAM
July brought the announcement that Hanoi wanted to accelerate the work on the MIA/POW issue to the point where it would be resolved within two years. U.S.-Vietnamese talks in Hanoi and New York then resulted in a plan for resolving the issue within two years. Additionally, the Vietnamese gave the United States permission to investigate the Yen Thuong crash site, with the investigation itself taking place in November. Prior to the investigation, the Vietnamese returned twenty-six sets of remains. Finally, as the year closed, another seven were returned.

LAOS
February saw an American-Laotian team investigate the Pakse site and remove the remains of its victims. U.S. delegations met with Laotian officials to discuss continued cooperation and to press for further crash-site investigations. At midyear, the Laotians agreed to an investigation of the Savannakhet site. Then, as the year closed, they pledged to allow further investigations in the future.

1986
VIETNAM
As a result of Hanoi's desire to resolve the MIA/POW issue within two years, three delegations visited the city in January and February, with the first being led by Mr. Armitage and the remaining two by congressional leaders. The Vietnamese

told the Armitage group that information was now being gathered on fifty more MIAs. When speaking to the second of the congressional groups, the Vietnamese revised the figure upward from fifty to seventy. Soon thereafter, they surrendered twenty-one sets of remains. Nine more sets were returned following an October technical meeting.

A series of technical meetings, plus talks between U.S. and Vietnamese officials, was held in the course of the year. Despite all the sessions and the increasing returns, President Reagan was troubled by what he saw as a slowing of Vietnam's effort to resolve the MIA/POW issue in two years' time. In part, the slowdown appeared to stem from Vietnamese annoyance over the fact that Washington, as it had long done, was insisting that a normalization of relations with Vietnam be contingent on Vietnamese troops leaving Cambodia.

The Vietnamese voiced their anger by accusing the United States of not being fully committed to the MIA/POW effort. To convince them of his serious intent, President Reagan decided to appoint a special MIA/POW envoy to Hanoi.

LAOS
The investigation of the Savannakhet site took place in February. U.S.-Laotian talks in New York City and Laos continued throughout the year. At one meeting, the United States again explained its reasons for suspecting that living MIAs might still be in Laos, held there as captives.

1987
VIETNAM
President Reagan made his appointment of the special MIA/POW envoy in February. Gen. John W. Vessey, Jr., a former chairman of the Joint Chiefs of Staff, was named as that envoy.

General Vessey met in Hanoi with Foreign Minister Thach, who was now also serving as the nation's prime minister. Thach agreed to resume Vietnam's cooperation in resolving the MIA/POW issue. General Vessey, for his part, agreed to have the United States address a number of Vietnamese humanitarian concerns, among them the need for medical assistance for the war's victims.

The Vessey-Thach meeting took place in August. A month later, the Vietnamese returned three sets of remains; they were identified as those of air force officers Maj. Roger E. Behnfelt, Lt. Col. Wayne Fullam, and Maj. Michael J. Bosiljevac (see chapter 6). Two sets were then returned in November and are still under study for identification at the time this book was being written.

LAOS

Meetings were held in Washington and Laos for the purpose of furthering U.S.-Laotian cooperation in the MIA/POW issue.

TODAY

The work done in the 1980s has alleviated somewhat the suspicion that Washington is still trying to "close the books" on the MIA/POW issue. Although many people now believe that a sincere effort is being made to resolve the issue, there are thousands who are impatient with the U.S.-Vietnamese negotiations, which seem slow moving (as virtually all diplomatic negotiations are) and too often interrupted by squabbles between the two countries. The result has been that the problem of the missing is still unresolved months after the two years that were to see its resolution have passed.

These feelings have prompted a number of recent actions by concerned Americans, both within and outside the government. The years 1986–1988 saw the following steps taken on behalf of the missing:

1986

H. Ross Perot, the Texas billionaire who founded Electronic Data Systems, took his concern for the missing directly to

President Reagan and demanded that he "get to the bottom" of the issue.[6]

In November former Green Beret officer James "Bo" Gritz returned to the headlines when he led a CBS television producer to Thailand to film a documentary on Americans still held prisoner in Laos. The Thai government, still angry at Gritz for using Thailand as the jumping-off point for his earlier forays into Laos, ordered him out of the country but allowed the producer to remain. A group of Americans then persuaded the British Broadcasting Corporation to film a documentary on the suspected POWs in Laos. The documentary, which was advertised as the story of "the men America left behind," was seen on a number of U.S. TV stations in January 1987.[7]

1987

In October a group of MIA families announced their plan to float thousands of balloons into Laos. The balloons were to carry messages offering money and a safe haven to anyone who brought an American out of the country.[8]

The year also saw Rep. Robert C. Smith of New Hampshire introduce into the U.S. House of Representatives a bill aimed against the Carter administration's long-ago order to "classify" information on the MIAs and POWs. His bill called for the information to be "declassified" so that, once again available to the press and public, it could be used to generate further interest in the MIA/POW issue.[9]

1988

In January three congressmen, Mr. Smith, John Rowland of Connecticut, and Frank McClosky of Indiana, flew to Southeast Asia for talks with Vietnamese officials about the missing and about the possibility of private aid being given to Vietnam's war victims. Their trip took them into Cambodia, where they discussed the eighty-two Americans who had vanished there during the war. A Cambodian official told them that his country holds the remains of eighty men and is willing to return them. The news was seen in the United States as either a propaganda move or an opening bid by Cambodia for improved relations with Washington.[10] The United States has maintained no diplomatic ties with Cambodia since the end of the Vietnam War.

In July, Vietnam and the United States announced that they planned to launch a joint mission to recover the remains of still-missing servicemen.[11] The search was expected to center on the sixty-five to seventy-four "most compelling" MIA cases that were discussed in chapter 4. The announcement raised hopes that the slowness that had marked the U.S.-Vietnam MIA negotiations was ending and that the issue would at last be resolved.

These hopes were soon shattered. In early August, Vietnam cancelled the planned mission. The Hanoi government angrily gave as its reason "the hostile policy" of the Reagan administration.

Behind Hanoi's anger was a July statement by an administration official. As you'll recall from chapter 6, the economically troubled Vietnamese have long wanted to establish normal relations with the United States, but President Reagan has always said that this could not be done until Vietnam removed its troops from Cambodia. Vietnam took a major step toward normalization in 1988 when it began to pull its troops out and announced that a total withdrawal would be completed in 1990. The administration official triggered Hanoi's ire when he came out against a proposed resolution by the U.S. Congress to establish low-level diplomatic ties—the first step towards full normalization—now that the Vietnamese troops were leaving Cambodia. He said that no U.S.-Vietnamese diplomatic ties should be established until the withdrawal was complete.

The decision to abandon the joint mission, however, proved to be a temporary one. Hanoi, with its desire for the establishment of normal relations with the United States obviously overriding its anger, reversed its position late in August. The Vietnamese government announced that it would resume work on the joint effort to find the still-missing Americans.

And so the 1980s have been marked throughout by diplomatic, congressional, and private actions on behalf of the missing. Though the U.S.-Vietnamese negotiations have been criticized for their slowness and despite the temporary trouble over the joint U.S.-Vietnamese search effort, there is no doubt that definite progress toward a resolution has been made. That progress is best seen in the increasing number of remains that have been returned since 1981.

Despite the progress recorded in the 1980s, the problem of the Vietnam missing continues to be a source of anguish for their families and of concern to Americans everywhere. It is to be hoped that the problem will soon be resolved and bring to an end the anguish and concern it has caused. Always remaining, however, will be a deep national sorrow for the missing of Vietnam and for the Americans who gave their lives there.

EPILOGUE

At the time this book was completed, 2,410 Americans remain unaccounted for in Southeast Asia. A state-by-state listing of their names is available upon request by writing to the National League of Families of American Prisoners and Missing in Southeast Asia, 1608 K Street, N.W., Washington, D.C., 20006.

NOTES

INTRODUCTION

1. The material on the history of the Vietnam War, and its causes and effects on the U.S. public, is developed from Frances Fitzgerald, *Fire in the Lake: The Vietnamese and the Americans in Vietnam* (Boston: Little, Brown, 1972), 66–67; 80; 85; 149; 303; Dennis Bloodworth, *An Eye for the Dragon: Southeast Asia Observed, 1954–1970* (New York: Farrar, Strauss and Giroux, 1970), 206; Edward F. Dolan, Jr., *Amnesty: The American Puzzle* (New York: Watts, 1976), 19–24; 27–36; John T. McAlister, Jr., *Viet Nam: The Origins of Revolution* (New York: Knopf, 1969), 351–365.

CHAPTER ONE

1. The three stories that open the chapter are developed from "Missing," *Life*, November 1987, 112–14.
2. The totals given for the missing and the locations in which they disappeared are derived from *Newsweek*, December 2, 1985, 60; *Life*, November 1987, 110; a letter to the author from the National League of Families of American Prisoners and Missing in Southeast Asia.

3. James Rosenthal, "The Myth of the Lost POWs," *New Republic*, July 1, 1985, 15.
4. "Vietnam: The Hunt for MIA's," *Newsweek*, December 2, 1985, 60.
5. "Tracking the Last MIA's," *Newsweek*, March 4, 1985, 37; Peter T. White, "Missing in Action," *National Geographic*, November 1986, 692; "Jungle Hunt for Missing Airmen," *Time*, February 25, 1985, 21.
6. From a conversation with Adrian Fisch, director, Red Badge of Courage.
7. *New Republic*, July 1, 1985, 15.
8. Paul A. Gigot, "Lost or Merely Forgotten?" *National Review*, August 17, 1979, 1035–36.
9. Material on the number of MIAs who may, in theory, still be alive in Southeast Asia is developed from *New Republic*, July 1, 1985, 15.
10. *Life*, November 1987, 114.
11. Thomas D. Boettcher and Joseph A. Rehyansky, "We Can Keep You . . . Forever," *National Review*, August 21, 1981, 962.
12. *Life*, November 1987, 114.
13. "Daring Mission, Dashed Hopes," *Time*, June 1, 1981, 31; Richard L. Berke, "POW's Alive in Vietnam, Report Concludes," *New York Times*, September 30, 1986; Robert Shaplen, *Bitter Victory* (New York: Harper & Row, 1986), 62.
14. *Newsweek*, December 2, 1985, 60.
15. *New Republic*, July 1, 1985, 17.
16. "U.N., North Korea Move Quietly on MIA Remains Issue," *Pittsburgh Press*, September 22, 1986; Bill Paul, "Pay for U.S. Prisoners in Communist Hands," *Wall Street Journal*, August 19, 1986.

CHAPTER TWO

1. Arnold R. Isaacs, *Without Honor* (Baltimore: Johns Hopkins University Press, 1983), 61.
2. The material on President Nixon's policy of Vietnamization and the signing of the peace pact is developed from Frances Fitzgerald, *Fire in the Lake: The Vietnamese and the Americans in Vietnam* (Boston: Little, Brown, 1972), 404–08; *Without Honor*, 61.
3. Gabriel Kolko, *Anatomy of a War* (New York: Pantheon, 1985), 611; *Without Honor*, 64.
4. The two agreements pertaining to POWs and MIAs are derived from *Without Honor*, 65.
5. Thomas D. Boettcher and Joseph A. Rehyansky, "We Can Keep You . . . Forever," *National Review*, August 21, 1981, 958; *Without Honor*, 131.
6. The material on the problems of the Four-Party Joint Military Team and the violations of the Paris peace pact is developed from *Without Honor*, 64–68; 131–33.

7. The material on the death of Captain Rees is developed from *Without Honor*, 132.
8. The material on the Cambodian and Laotian fighting is developed from *Without Honor*, 67; 134–35.
9. The material on President Nixon's proffered $3.25 billion in aid is developed from *Anatomy of a War*, 447; *Without Honor*, 133–34.
10. *Without Honor*, 131–32.
11. *Without Honor*, 132.
12. *Without Honor*, 137.

CHAPTER THREE

1. Thomas D. Boettcher and Joseph A. Rehyansky, "We Can Keep You . . . Forever," *National Review*, August 21, 1981, 960.
2. The material on the House Select Committee on Missing Persons in Southeast Asia and the general criticisms with which its report was received is developed from *National Review*, August 21, 1981, 961; James Rosenthal, "The Myth of the Lost POWs," *New Republic*, July 1, 1985, 18.
3. Paul A. Gigot, "Lost or Merely Forgotten?" *National Review*, August 17, 1979, 1036.
4. "Missing," *Life*, November 1987, 113.
5. *National Review*, August 21, 1981, 959.
6. The material on the National League of Families and its objections to the House Select Committee's report is developed from information provided by the league's headquarters, Washington, D.C.
7. *National Review*, August 17, 1979, 1037 (Gougglemann); *National Review*, August 21, 1981, 961 (Gougglemann and Gay).
8. The material on the objections to the House Select Committee's report from within the committee is developed from "Why—Mr. President?" a radio address by Lt. Col. (Ret.) Starr W. Jones, prepared for broadcast on Boston station WHET in September 1977.
9. Arnold R. Isaacs, *Without Honor* (Baltimore: Johns Hopkins University Press, 1983), 134–35.
10. *New Republic*, July 1, 1985, 18.
11. "Daring Mission, Dashed Hopes," *Time*, June 1, 1981, 31.

CHAPTER FOUR

1. The totals given for the sightings of living Americans in Southeast Asia are derived from "Exploiting the MIA Families?" *Newsweek*, April 11, 1983, 34; James Rosenthal, "The Myth of the Lost POWs," *New Republic*, July 1, 1985, 15; "Missing," *Life*, November 1987, 114.

2. "Daring Mission, Dashed Hopes," *Time,* June 1, 1981, 31; "A Secret Mission to Search for MIA's," *Newsweek,* June 1, 1981, 54.
3. Bill Paul, "POWs Won't Be Found Without Cost," *Wall Street Journal,* April 24, 1985.
4. Thomas D. Boettcher and Joseph A. Rehyansky, "We Can Keep You . . . Forever," *National Review,* August 21, 1981, 961.
5. Bob Poos, "POWs: Pawns of War," *Vietnam,* a publication of *Soldier of Fortune* magazine, February 1986, 83–84.
6. "The Lost Americans," *Newsweek,* January 20, 1986, 26.
7. *Life,* November 1987, 116.
8. Paul A. Gigot, "Lost or Merely Forgotten?" *National Review,* August 17, 1979, 1038.
9. *Wall Street Journal,* April 24, 1985.
10. *Vietnam,* 83.
11. Bill Paul, "POWs: The Evidence Is There; Now Let's Act," *Wall Street Journal,* April 21, 1986.
12. *Vietnam,* 84.
13. The material on the operation of the Defense Intelligence Agency is developed from *National Review,* August 21, 1981, 961; *Life,* November 1987, 116.
14. *Newsweek,* April 11, 1983, 34.
15. *New Republic,* July 1, 1985, 15.
16. All figures pertaining to the resolution of the reported sightings on record by 1987 are developed from "League Positions," an informational bulletin by the National League of Families, May 1, 1987.
17. *Life,* November 1987, 111.
18. *Wall Street Journal,* April 24, 1985.

CHAPTER FIVE

1. Thomas D. Boettcher and Joseph A. Rehyansky, "We Can Keep You . . . Forever," *National Review,* August 21, 1981, 962.
2. "Missing," *Life,* November 1987, 111; *National Review,* August 21, 1981, 962.
3. *National Review,* August 21, 1981, 960.
4. Ibid.
5. *Life,* November 1987, 113.
6. *National Review,* August 21, 1981, 958.
7. *National Review,* August 21, 1981, 958–59.
8. *Life,* November 1987, 113.
9. "Inside Vietnam: What a Former POW Found," *U.S. News & World Report,* March 11, 1985, 33.
10. The material for the story of Captain Estocin is developed from *Life,* November 1987, 116.

11. The material for the "52" mystery is developed from "Daring Mission, Dashed Hopes," *Times*, June 1, 1981, 31; "A Secret Mission to Search for MIA's," *Newsweek*, June 1, 1981, 54.
12. *National Review*, August 21, 1981, 960.

CHAPTER SIX

1. "Still Missing," *Life*, July 1986, 39.
2. "The Search for Missing Servicemen," *Newsweek*, November 10, 1980, 16–17; Thomas D. Boettcher and Joseph A. Reyhansky, "We Can Keep You . . . Forever," *National Review*, August 21, 1981, 961.
3. James L. Pate, "Missing in Action," *Soldier of Fortune*, July 1986, 33.
4. The statement that 173 sets of MIA remains have been identified plus the subsequent listing of the years in which the identifications were made are derived from information provided by the National League of Families.
5. Josh Getlin, "Hearts and Bones," *Los Angeles Times Magazine*, October 12, 1986, 26.
6. From an interview with Colleen Shine, public affairs coordinator, the National League of Families, February 8, 1988.
7. From information provided by the National League of Familes.
8. "Exploiting the MIA Families?" *Newsweek*, April 11, 1983, 34.
9. "Recent High Level Government Commitments," an informational bulletin by the National League of Families, undated.
10. The material of Vietnam's economy is developed from "The Lost Americans," *Newsweek*, January 20, 1986, 27; "Inside Vietnam: What A Former POW Found," *U.S. News & World Report*, March 11, 1985, 33; "MIA's: A Surprise from Hanoi," *Newsweek*, July 22, 1985, 34.
11. *Newsweek*, January 20, 1986, 26.
12. The material on the events in Cambodia is developed from François Ponchaud, *Cambodia: Year Zero* (New York: Holt, Rinehart and Winston, 1977), 1–2; 52–71; 82–83; Stanley Karnow, *Vietnam: A History—The First Complete Account of Vietnam at War* (New York: Viking Press, 1983), 685–86; Arnold R. Isaacs, *Without Honor* (Baltimore: Johns Hopkins University Press, 1983), 285–89; "Thailand Acts on Refugees," *Facts on File*, April 26, 1975; "Cambodians in Retreat," *Facts on File*, January 1–5, 1979, 1; "U.S. Arms Arrive in Thailand," *Facts on File*, July 11, 1980, 508.
13. *Newsweek*, July 22, 1985, 34.
14. *Newsweek*, January 20, 1986, 26.
15. *Newsweek*, July 22, 1986, 34.
16. Nick B. Williams, "Hanoi Tells of Losses in Cambodia" (reprinted from the *Los Angeles Times*), *San Francisco Chronicle*, July 1, 1988.
17. "Jungle Hunt for Missing Americans," *Time*, February 25, 1985, 21.
18. The material on foreign ministry official Cuu Dinh Ba and Vietnam's

desire to "accelerate" the resolution of the MIA issue is developed from *Newsweek*, July 22, 1985, 34.

19. "Vietnam to U.S.—26 More Coffins," *U.S. News & World Report*, August 26, 1985, 9.

CHAPTER SEVEN

1. The material on unidentified and identified bones is developed from "Still Missing," *Life*, July, 1986, 39; Josh Getlin, "Hearts and Bones," *Los Angeles Times Magazine*, October 12, 1986, 15; information bulletin, National League of Families, October 1987.
2. The material on the NLF visit to the Pakse site and then the Laotian permission to investigate the site is developed from "Jungle Hunt for Missing Americans," *Time*, February 25, 1985, 21.
3. James Willwerth, "Excavating the Recent Past," *Time*, March 4, 1985, 49.
4. *Time*, March 4, 1985, 49.
5. The material on the investigation of the Pakse site is developed from "Tracking the Last MIA's," *Newsweek*, March 4, 1985, 37; James L. Pate, "Missing in Action," *Soldier of Fortune*, July 1986, 32; *Time*, February 25, 1985, 21; *Time*, March 4, 1985, 49; *Los Angeles Times Magazine*, October 12, 1986, 15.
6. The material on the investigation of the Savannakhet site is developed from Peter T. White, "Missing in Action," *National Geographic*, November 1986, 692–96; information bulletin, National League of Families, October 1987.
7. The material on the investigaton of the Yen Thuong site is developed from "Vietnam: The Hunt for MIA's," *Newsweek*, December 2, 1985, 60.
8. The material on the Hart case is developed from *Los Angeles Times Magazine*, October 12, 1986, 14–15; 24.
9. The material on the Fuller case is developed from *Life*, July 1986, 42; *Los Angeles Times Magazine*, October 12, 1986, 24; *Soldier of Fortune*, July 1986, 35–36.
10. The material on the Fanning case is developed from *Life*, July 1986, 41.
11. Ibid.
12. The material on the investigation of the Central Identification Laboratory is developed from *Los Angeles Times Magazine*, October 12, 1986, 15; 26–27; *Soldier of Fortune*, July 1986, 34–36.

CHAPTER EIGHT

1. The material on the Woodcock Commission is developed from Paul A. Gigot, "Lost or Merely Forgotten?" *National Review*, August 17, 1979,

1036–37; Thomas D. Boettcher and Joseph A. Reyhansky, "We Can Keep You . . . Forever," *National Review,* August 21, 1981, 959.

2. "Exploiting the MIA Families," *Newsweek,* April 11, 1983, 34.

3. Ibid.

4. The material on the Gritz rescue missions is developed from *Newsweek,* April 11, 1983, 34; "Daring Mission, Dashed Hopes," *Time,* June 1, 1981, 31; "Colonel Gritz's Dubious Mission," *Time,* April 4, 1983, 33.

5. The material on the U.S. negotiations with Vietnam and Laos is developed from an informational bulletin headed "POW/MIA Briefing," August 1987; "Chronology of US/SRV POW/MIA Activities," undated; "Chronology of US/LAOS Relations," undated—all issued by the National League of Families.

6. Bill Paul, "Activists Bid to Free Any POWs Still in Asia Stir Hopes and Doubts," *Wall Street Journal,* January 21, 1987.

7. Ibid.

8. "Balloons Sent Out for MIAs," *San Francisco Sunday Examiner,* October 11, 1987.

9. "DIA Releases Names of POW Cases After 14 Years," *Stars and Stripes,* October 12, 1987.

10. "Congressmen Talk to Hanoi Officials," *San Francisco Chronicle,* January 9, 1988; "Cambodia Says It Has Bodies of 80 Americans," *San Francisco Chronicle,* January 18, 1988.

11. The material on the planned U.S.-Vietnamese search for MIAs is developed from: "U.S., Vietnam Set to Hunt MIAs Together" (reprinted from the *Los Angeles Times*), *San Francisco Chronicle,* July 22, 1988; "Vietnam Pulls Out of Search for MIAs" (reprinted from the *Washington Post*), *San Francisco Chronicle,* August 4, 1988; Steven Erlanger, "Missing in Action: From a Lost War, a Haunting Echo That Won't Be Stilled," *The New York Times,* August 31, 1988.

BIBLIOGRAPHY

BOOKS

Bloodworth, Dennis. *An Eye for the Dragon: Southeast Asia Observed, 1954–1970.* New York: Farrar, Strauss and Giroux, 1970.

Dolan, Jr., Edward F. *Amnesty: The American Puzzle.* New York: Franklin Watts, 1976.

Edelman, Bernard, editor for the New York Veterans Memorial Commission. *Dear America: Letters Home from Vietnam.* New York: W. W. Norton, 1985.

Fincher, E. B. *The Vietnam War.* New York: Franklin Watts, 1980.

Fitzgerald, Frances. *Fire in the Lake: The Vietnamese and the Americans in Vietnam.* Boston: Little, Brown and Company, 1972.

Isaacs, Arnold R. *Without Honor: Defeat in Vietnam and Cambodia.* Baltimore: Johns Hopkins University Press, 1983.

Karnow, Stanley. *Vietnam: A History—The First Complete Account of Vietnam at War.* New York: Viking Press, 1983.

Kolko, Gabriel. *Anatomy of a War: Vietnam, the United States, and the Modern Historical Experience.* New York: Pantheon Books, 1985.

Lawson, Don. *The War in Vietnam.* New York: Franklin Watts, 1981.

Mabie, Margaret C. J. *Vietnam: There and Here.* New York: Holt, Rinehart and Winston, 1985.

McAlister, Jr., John T. *Viet Nam: The Origins of Revolution*. New York: Alfred A. Knopf, 1969.

Ponchaud, François. *Cambodia: Year Zero*. New York: Holt, Rinehart and Winston, 1977.

Salisbury, Harrison, editor. *Vietnam Reconstructed: Lessons from a War*. New York: Harper & Row, 1984.

Santoli, Al. *To Bear Any Burden: The Vietnam War and its Aftermath in the Words of Americans and Southeast Asians*. New York: E. P. Dutton, 1985.

Scholl-Latour, Robert. *Death in the Rice Fields: An Eyewitness Account of Vietnam's Three Wars, 1945–1970*. New York: St. Martin's Press, 1979.

Shaplen, Robert. *Bitter Victory*. New York: Harper & Row, 1986.

—— *The Road From War: Vietnam 1965–1970*. New York: Harper & Row, 1970.

Trager, Frank N. *Why Vietnam?* New York: Frederick A. Praeger, 1966.

MAGAZINE ARTICLES

Beck, Melinda. "Exploiting the MIA Families," *Newsweek*, April 11, 1983.

Boettcher, Thomas D. and Rehyansky, Joseph A. "We Can Keep You . . . Forever," *National Review*, August 21, 1981.

Deming, Angus. "MIA's: A Surprise from Hanoi," *Newsweek*, July 22, 1985.

—— "The Rambo Syndrome: Are Some MIA's Still POWs?" *Newsweek*, January 20, 1986.

—— "Vietnam: The Hunt for MIA's," *Newsweek*, December 2, 1985.

Fineman, Howard. "Laos: A Secret Mission to Search for MIA's," *Newsweek*, June 1, 1981.

Gigot, Paul A. "Lost or Merely Forgotten?" *National Review*, August 17, 1979.

Henry, William A. "Daring Mission, Dashed Hopes," *Time*, June 1, 1981.

Hitchens, Christopher. "Minority Report," *The Nation*, June 14, 1986.

Iyer, Pico. "Colonel Gritz's Dubious Mission," *Time*, April 4, 1983.

Life. "Still Missing: The Search for Vietnam's War Dead Takes Puzzling New Turns," July, 1986.

Life. "Missing," November, 1987.

McManus, John F. "Americans in the Gulag: Our Countrymen Are Held Throughout the Communist World," *The New American*, December 8, 1986.

Newsweek. "The Search for Missing Servicemen," November 10, 1980.

Newsweek. "Tracking the Last MIA's," March 4, 1985.

Pate, James L. "Missing in Action," *Soldier of Fortune*, July, 1986.

Poos, Bob. "POW/MIAs: Pawns of War," *Vietnam,* a publication of *Soldier of Fortune* magazine, February, 1986.

Rosenthal, James. "The Myth of the Lost POWs," *The New Republic,* July 1, 1985.

U.S. News & World Report. "Inside Vietnam: What A Former POW Found," March 11, 1985.

U.S. News & World Report. "Vietnam to U.S.—26 More Coffins," August 26, 1985.

U.S. News & World Report. "POW's in Vietnam: Fact or Fiction?" October 28, 1985.

Whitaker, Mary. "The Lost Americans," *Newsweek,* January 20, 1986.

White, Peter T. "Missing in Action," *The National Geographic,* November, 1986.

Willwerth, James. "Excavating the Recent Past," *Time,* March 4, 1985.

Zintl, Robert T. "Jungle Hunt for Missing Airmen," *Time,* February 25, 1985.

NEWSPAPER ARTICLES

Berke, Richard L. "P.O.W.'s Alive in Vietnam, Report Concludes," *The New York Times,* September 30, 1986.

Foisie, Jack. "Relations Thawing with Vietnam," *San Francisco Chronicle,* January 14, 1988.

Getlin, Josh. "Hearts and Bones," *Los Angeles Times Magazine,* October 12, 1986.

Gottlieb, Henry. "U.S.—Laos," Associated Press release, August 20, 1987.

Paul, Bill. "POWs Won't be Found Without Cost," *The Wall Street Journal,* April 24, 1985.

———— "McFarlane Believes Some U.S. POWs Are in Indochina," *The Wall Street Journal,* October 15, 1985.

———— "POWs: The Evidence Is There; Now Let's Act," *The Wall Street Journal,* April 21, 1986.

———— "Pay for U.S. Prisoners in Communist Hands," *The Wall Street Journal,* August 19, 1986.

———— "Activists' Bids to Free Any POWs Still in Asia Stir Hopes and Doubts," *The Wall Street Journal,* January 21, 1987.

INDEX